CONCILIUM

CONCILIUM 2012/1

SACRAMENTALIZING HUMAN HISTORY

In Honour of Edward Schillebeeckx (1914–2009)

Edited by

Erik Borgman, Paul D. Murray, and
Andrés Torres Queiruga

SCM Press · London

Published in 2012 by SCM Press, 13–17 Long Lane, London EC1A 9PN

SCM Press is an imprint of Hymns Ancient & Modern Ltd (a registered charity)
13A Hellesdon Park Road, Norwich NR6 5DR, UK

www.concilium.in

ISBN 978 0 334 03117 8

Printed in the UK by
CPI Group (UK) Ltd, Croydon, CR0 4YY

Concilium is published in March, June, August, October, December

Contents

Part Two: Theological Forum

Editorial

On 23 December 2009, after a short illness, the theologian and Dominican Edward Schillebeeckx died in Nijmegen, where he had lived. Edward Cornelis Florent Alfons Schillebeeckx was the sixth of 14 children and first saw light on 12 November 1914 in Antwerp, while his family was displaced by the First World War, recently launched. Edward entered the Dominican Order in Flanders, taught at the Dominican study house in Leuven, became professor for Dogmatics and the History of Theology at the University of Nijmegen in 1957, and stayed in Nijmegen until his retirement in 1983. He was one of the major Catholic theologians of the twentieth century, an important figure at Vatican II,[3] and one of the founders of *Concilium* in 1964. Schillebeeckx was deeply involved in the debates on the profile and strategy of the journal throughout the decennia. He helped to keep the Secretariat in Nijmegen running. Between 1965 and 1997, Schillebeeckx wrote 18 articles for *Concilium.* However, if we dedicate this issue on the sacraments and the sacramentality of human history to the honour of Schillebeeckx, it is not a nostalgic gesture. We think that Schillebeeckx's theological vision is important for the future of theology.

As one of the founders of *Concilium,* Edward Schillebeeckx wrote, together with Karl Rahner, the 'General Introduction' for the journal, published in the first issue in 1965. The theology *Concilium* aimed to develop was characterized as follows:

> Quite clearly [. . .] it is deliberately based on Scripture and the history of salvation. At the same time it has the humble courage to confront the new problems arising from the human conditions of today. It seeks, on the basis of our contemporary situation, a better understanding of the Word of God for man and the world of our time. A theological insight of this kind is necessary for anyone who, acting in faith, is actively engaged in the Church and in the world.

Seeking a fuller understanding of the Word of God for human beings as a way to understand the world of our time better, and the other way around, has always been characteristic of Schillebeeckx's theology. He did not aim at applying or translating the tradition to the present, he wanted to read the present theologically, as a time and a place of God's presence. Reflection on the sacraments and sacramentality, which was both the topic of his first theological book and his last major theological article, was an important way for him to realize this aim. Since the mid-1960s, Schillebeeckx first of all related God to the future given to us. This suggests that the sacraments need to be understood in reference to what human beings and communities could become, opening up before us a world of new possibilities. In Schillebeeckx's view, God comes to us anew each moment in liberating occurrences and experiences that sacramentalize history as the space of God's revelation.

Schillebeeckx's renewed reflections on the sacraments were still developing when he was forced to admit that he would be unable to finish them. This issue of *Concilium* is a modest attempt to contribute to the future of this project.

The issue opens with an article by Erik Borgman (Tilburg, The Netherlands) on Schillebeeckx's development and how the sacramentality of and sacramentalizing human history are central topics in his *œuvre.* For Aquinas, sacraments signify and embody the presence of God's salvation, and according to Schillebeeckx, this is not limited to the history of Jesus. God's real presence is among us in our everyday lives: it is an important intuition, but Schillebeeckx did not fully develop it. Jennifer Cooper (Oxford, Great Britain) analyses Schillebeeckx's theology of the Eucharist as a way in which believers participate in the salvific presence of God to the world. Andrés Torres Queiruga (Santiago, Spain) develops an understanding of the sacraments as living celebrations that with their symbolism help believers to be aware of and open to the always active presence of God in vital situations. Thus they are real and transforming events of grace, and not, as they often were and are seen among Catholics, words and acts with a quasi-magical efficacy.

Johnson Siluvaipillai (Tiruchirapalli, India) sees the sacraments as celebrations of the kenotic commitment of Jesus Christ on earth. Through them, the believing community is propelled to engage itself with the Other in order to experience the divine grace. Ben Kautzer (Durham, Great Britain) investigates what it would mean not so much to understand the liturgy as a source for ethics, but to understand ethical acts in the mundane, everyday world liturgically, not producing but symbolizing

God's coming reign. Paul D. Murray (Durham, Great Britain) discusses Schillebeeckx's ecclesiology as a challenging attempt to break away from theological abstraction and a plea to turn to the lived experience of ecclesial reality in the midst of concrete historical contexts. He feels we should go further along the way than Schillebeeckx himself in fact did. Stephan van Erp (Nijmegen, The Netherlands) closes the thematic section on sacramentalizing human history by developing a view on the future of the main impulses in Edward Schillebeeckx's theological project. Incarnation and sacramentality will be the key concepts, in his view.

Liturgical reforms coming from the church hierarchy seem to run counter to what Schillebeeckx tried to develop when he was thinking about the sacraments and their meaning and significance. In the Theological Forum there are two rather different articles on the occasion of the introduction of the new translation of the Roman Missal for the English-speaking world, starting the first Sunday of Advent 2011. Kevin T. Kelly (Liverpool, Great Britain) protests the way the translation was produced and promulgated, without any input from people representing the local churches or a pastoral approach. Joseph Lionel (Bangalore, India) debates the concept of continuity on which much of the discussions on the liturgy since Vatican II is based. He pleads for multidimensional research on continuity and discontinuity in the liturgical tradition of the Church.

Sadly, in many places the Roman Catholic Church is involved in investigations on sex abuse of minors by its clergy. From the debates taking place in the Netherlands, Erik Borgman presents some of the theological questions the sexual abuse crisis brings to the fore.

We thank Susan Ross (Chicago, USA) and Felix Wilfred (Chennai, India) for their advice regarding this issue.

Erik Borgman, Paul D. Murray, Andrés Torres Queiruga

Notes

1. Edward Schillebeeckx, *De sacramentele heilseconomie: Theologische bezinning op S. Thomas' sacramentenleer in het licht van de traditie en van de hedendaagse sacramentsproblematiek* I, Antwerp: 't Groeit/Bilthoven: Nelissen, 1952, p. 140.
2. Edward Schillebeeckx, 'Sacramenteel leven', *Thomas* 3 (1949–50) no. 3, 5–6, here 5; quoted in E. Borgman, *Edward Schillebeeckx: A Theologian in His History* Part I: *A Catholic Theology of Culture (1914–1965)*, London/New York: Continuum, 2003, pp. 209–10.
3. Cf. Karim Schelkens, *The Council Diaries of Edward Schillebeeckx, 1962–1963* (Critically annotated Bilingual Edition), Leuven: Peeters, 2010.

Part One: Sacramentalizing Human History

Edward Schillebeeckx's Reflections on the Sacraments and the Future of Catholic Theology

ERIK BORGMAN

During the homily I had the honour to give at Edward Schillebeeckx's Funeral Mass in Nijmegen on 31 December 2009, I reminded the congregation that, in his own view, his theology was unfinished as he died, just before Christmas. Already in his eighties, in the late 1990s, Schillebeeckx developed the plan to rewrite his first book, *De Sacramentele Heilseconomie* [The Sacramental Economy of Salvation], published in Dutch in 1952.[1] As translations of this book were non-existent for a long time, Karl Rahner wrote that every theologian should learn Dutch to read it, and he seems to have done so himself. However, it was not nostalgia for his early success that brought Schillebeeckx back to the topic of the book that had been his dissertation for the Master's Degree (*Sacra Theologiae Magister*) in the Dominican Order. Although it was somewhat of a coincidence that Schillebeeckx took the sacraments as the topic for his thesis, rather than one of the other dogmatic topics on which he produced extensive lecture notes during his years as a professor at the Dominican *Studium* in Leuven – such as the theology of creation, on which he developed a highly innovative view – the topic kept fascinating him for the rest of his life.[2]

In the 1990s, Schillebeeckx came into contact with the relatively new field of Ritual Studies. He decided that he had fundamentally to re-think the whole subject of sacramentality in terms of the concept of ritualization. In 2000, he tried to put all his thoughts on the subject together in one long article, published in *Tijdschrift voor Theologie,* the journal he had founded in 1960.[3] The subtitle was telling: 'Ritualizing Religious Elements in Daily Life'. It was his interpretation of the core of Ritual Studies, which sees ritualizing as a human process in which certain aspect of daily life are celebrated, set apart, and thus sanctified. It would help him, Schillebeeckx thought, to draw the consequences of the theological development of the decennia after the Second Vatican Council. As it turned out, however, shortly after 2000, Schillebeeckx was obliged to accept that his energy and ability to concentrate did not allow for the writing of another major work.

Yet he had envisaged something important. In this article, I present the theological development of the later Schillebeeckx through the lens of his views on the sacraments. I will argue that his approach is ultimately helpful for understanding human history as sacramental, and that such an understanding can give an important new impulse to contemporary Catholic theology.

I Sacramental encounter with God

Schillebeeckx's thesis in *De Sacramentele Heilseconomie* was already that sacraments were not something special in and of themselves. What is special about the sacraments is not certain particular characteristics of the rituals of Eucharist, Confession, Baptism, Confirmation, Marriage, Ordination, and the Anointing of the Sick. What is special about the sacraments is what, as *signs* – '*sacramentum est in genere signum*', Schillebeeckx quoted Thomas Aquinas – they are signs *of* and are pointing *to* the saving history of God's presence in Jesus Christ.[4] In and by the Sacraments, the living Christ remains present in his Church and to the world, in Schillebeeckx's view.

From his mentors in the Dominican 'wing' of *nouvelle theologie* during the 1940s and 50s, Marie-Dominique Chenu (1895–1990) and Yves Congar (1904–95), Schillebeeckx had learned that God is not present to the world only in and through the Church. It is God's continuing presence to the world that is perceived, expressed, and thus reinforced by the Church. Following Henri-Dominique Lacordaire (1802–60), Chenu and Congar shared the view of the 1950s Worker Priests in France that *presence au monde est presence à Dieu:* presence in the world is presence with God. This is what Vatican II was to express in its dogmatic constitution on the Church, *Lumen Gentium,* with the phrase that the Church is 'a sacrament'. The Church, the Council Fathers formulated, is 'a sign and instrument [. . .] of communion with

God and of the unity of the entire human race' (no. 1). In this the Church follows Christ, who was himself the sacramental encounter with God, as Schillebeeckx had argued since the late 1950s.[5]

But what exactly is the encounter with God that Jesus Christ embodies? And how is that related to our encounter with God? It is on these questions that Schillebeeckx intensively reflected in the years after the Council, which resulted in the books that made him a truly universal theologian: *Jesus an Experiment in Christology* (Dutch: *Jezus, het verhaal van een levende,* 1974) and *Christ the Experience of Jesus as Lord* (Dutch: *Gerechtigheid en liefde: Genade en bevrijding,* 1977). In them he examined the question of the continuity between the Jesus of history and the Christ proclaimed by the Church, breaking away from the assumption that – because the Church defines it to be so – the Jesus of Nazareth whom the faithful confessed to be salvation from God is the same as the Christ the Church through the centuries offered and offers now to the world for its salvation. The continuity is what matters, for if the Saviour and the Son of God the Church confesses has nothing to do with the Jesus that walked upon this earth, Christianity becomes nothing more than an unhistorical 'myth' that has lost its specific and critical meaning, Schillebeeckx stated: 'If we ask what is meant by the "eschatological salvation" given to us by the crucified-and-risen One, to give substance and content to this we have to point to Jesus of Nazareth himself, his person and his whole career and course of action up to and including his death'.[5]

Schillebeeckx's aim, however, was not to found the Christian faith on the 'historical Jesus'. He emphasized that, just like the 'dogmatic Christ' constructed by theology, the Jesus reconstructed by historical research is an abstraction, determined in this case by the possibilities and limits of the historical methods.[6] Christian faith on the other hand is, for Schillebeeckx, ultimately about a personal encounter with a concrete human being. Why and how a person is encouraged to see a 'Parable of God' in Jesus in such an encounter remains a mystery which can ultimately not be justified theoretically.[7] The concrete situation of the person who experiences the encounter is part of the encounter itself, Schillebeeckx argued, and this is in accordance with his hermeneutical concept of faith. He always realized that his Christology was also very much connected to his own historical situation. It was tied to the mentality of the 1970s and oriented toward reforming the world in the image of the Kingdom of God by active solidarity with the poor and the excluded.[8] But the fact that it was historically and socially situated was not a flaw in a theological project. It is exactly through this kind of contemporary incarnation that Christian faith shows its relevance and credibility, according to Schillebeeckx.

Simplifying a little, Schillebeeckx's Christology is mainly aimed at bridging a double chasm. First, he wants to show that it is possible reasonably to account for the transition from a faith in Jesus' message to a faith in Jesus as the Christ and the Son of God. Faith in Jesus as Christ is not opposed to Jesus' faith in the Kingdom of God, but its extension. According to Schillebeeckx, Jesus' message and life were based on a close relationship to God as his 'Abba'. That is why the rejection that was implied in his death on the cross demanded a corrective confirmation by God: the apparent break with what Jesus had turned into a final prophetic sign of faith by voluntarily submitting to it had to be healed by God. This is what happens in Jesus' resurrection and his ascension, and it is reaffirmed by the faithful when they confess Jesus as Christ and the beloved Son of God. Second, Schillebeeckx attempted to show that anyone who says he or she is no longer a believer, yet who feels inspired by the person of Jesus, is not as different from the believing Christian as either of them might think. The aspects of Jesus that appeal to the faithful are comparable to the inspiration non-Christians derive from him, Schillebeeckx argued.

II Ongoing incarnation

There is a third chasm that features in Schillebeeckx's work: the chasm between Jesus as a child of his time and the way the New Testament talks about him, and twentieth-century men and women as children of their time, to whom that same Jesus can still become a means of salvation and of redemption. Like many of his contemporaries, Schillebeeckx is often believed to have been concerned with the crossing of this gap, and sometimes Schillebeeckx himself suggests as much, but that is a highly misleading view. It is of the utmost importance to see how Schillebeeckx's vision differed fundamentally from the approach most prominent in the followers of Bultmann's 'de-mythologization' agenda. According to Schillebeeckx, we do not need a special method to free Jesus from his captivity in a mythical view of the world that, for instance, allows for direct divine intervention in history and even considers this to be likely. According to Bultmann and his disciples, our fundamental break with this worldview – not just theoretically but also and mainly practically: our use of electricity and radio, our faith in modern medicine – makes Jesus' message and acts irrelevant and obsolete, and it requires a special process of demythologization to recover this relevance.[9] However, it is typical of Schillebeeckx that is his view the chasm between present and past is continually bridged – whenever people testify to having been appealed to by Jesus, the message he preached, and the life he lived.

The 1960s and 70s witnessed a minor 'boom' in new, popular interpretations of Jesus, showing that he was of evident interest to contemporary people.[10] For Schillebeeckx, the fact that Jesus' message and actions can still be regarded as redeeming by his contemporaries is a confirmation of the Christian confession that he is still the Living One. Schillebeeckx is often misunderstood here. His point is *not* that Jesus lives on in the inspiration people receive from him throughout the ages, which would be in line with some of Bultmann's more radical disciples, who adhered to the idea that Jesus was resurrected and lived on in the proclamation that he was resurrected and lives on. Immediately after the publication of *Jesus an Experiment in Christology*, there was a considerable debate on whether Schillebeeckx fully confessed the real resurrection of Jesus. As a response he added five pages to the third edition of the Dutch edition of the book in 1975. In this passage, he explains extensively that this divine correction of Jesus' rejection implies that the same Jesus who was killed does truly live thanks to God. Schillebeeckx summarizes this as follows:

> Jesus' resurrection, acknowledged and confessed in and through the apostolic conversion or Easter experience, is: (a) God's legitimation, ratifying and sanctifying of Jesus' person, message and life of service 'unto death'; (b) it is also exaltation and new creation, that is to say, God's *corrective* triumph over the negativity of death and man's history of suffering, in which Jesus participated; in other words, there is life after death; (c) the resurrection is at the same time the sending of the Spirit and, in being that, the founding of the Church, a living fellowship, now renewed, of the personal, living Jesus Christ with his people on earth.[11]

So for Schillebeeckx, Jesus' resurrection is not identical to the news that his message goes on. It is the other way round in his view: the ongoing inspirational force people experience as coming from his life and message, even if they consider themselves non-believers, signifies Jesus' continuing presence among us.

III Retrieval or renewal

In his Christology, Schillebeeckx tried to show that there is no break between Jesus' historical existence (to the extent it can be established by means of the historical-critical method) and the believer's confession that he is God's Christ. Therefore all the emphasis is upon the fact that what was later said about Jesus can be regarded as the effect of the revelatory force that emanated from him during his life. According to Schillebeeckx, the 'history of God with man in Jesus, handed on and put into practice by the "community of God"', consisting of believers, is a 'history without a historical end', which continues at least until today.[12] In his view, it is the revelatory force that lay hidden in Jesus' verbal and practical preaching of the Kingdom of God by means of his historical words and acts that can still be felt in our day and age when people confess it in one way or another.

There is a problem hidden in all this, however. This can probably best be illustrated by the way Schillebeeckx treats the stories of the apparitions of Jesus after his death and resurrection. According to Schillebeeckx, what Jesus' disciples experience at Easter is that they are being converted, by Jesus' initiative, to Jesus as Christ and thereby finding definitive salvation in him.[13] The content of this conversion is that they return to doing what they did before, something they had erroneously allowed themselves to be distracted from by their failure and guilt: recognizing salvation as coming from God in the acts and words of Jesus during his lifetime. In Schillebeeckx's view, the stories of the apparitions of the Risen One are ultimately stories of repentance and confession by his disciples.

Now it is obviously beyond the scope of this article to develop a different exegesis of these stories. Yet it could be argued that Schillebeeckx does not fully do justice to the renewing expectation-bursting aspects of the actions of the Risen One in these stories. Rather than referring back to past actions, the apparition stories, like those about the Holy Spirit in the Acts of the Apostles, seem to express and stress that what has started with and in Jesus' life begins to create history in new and unprecedented ways after his death. The Gospel of Mark as a whole is entitled: 'The *beginning* of the Gospel of Jesus Christ, the Son of God' (1.1), and at the original ending of that Gospel (16.1–8), the women at the grave are told to go to Galilee, not in order to remember better what Jesus did there, but to meet him there anew. The famous words of the risen Jesus in the Gospel of John to Mary Magdalene, 'Do not hold on to me' (20.17), exhorts her to be open to new images from him revealed in new encounters. In Acts, the mission that Jesus started within the borders of Palestine expands to the ends of the earth.[14] All this does *not* suggest, I think, that the Church as the community of believers lives exclusively or mainly on what it has received through Jesus' words and actions in his history and through God's affirmation of them. In other words, faith is *not* simply about the 'story of God with people in Jesus, handed on and practised by the "communion of God"'.

Interestingly enough, Schillebeeckx has always strongly emphasized that, from a Christian point of view, the fullness of God's presence is not to be found in the past or the present, but in the future.[15] It is therefore rather strange that he clings so strongly to Jesus and his past history as our only point of contact with God's revelation. The task of the Church, in his view, is to hand on what has happened in and through Jesus as the Christ. At one point in his career, this very scheme seems to have brought him even to the brink of a crisis. In the introduction to *Church the Human Story of God,* the third part of his trilogy on Christology (Dutch: *Mensen als verhaal van God*, 1989), Schillebeeckx explained why he had not written the book he had envisaged as the sequel to *Jesus* and *Christ*. He had intended to publish a book about the Church as the historical and institutional embodiment of Jesus' message. However, he wrote, '[d]elight in belonging to this Church, a delight which increased greatly during the Second Vatican Council and the years immediately following, has been sorely tested over the last decade'.[16]

This mirrored the dominant mood at the time among Dutch Catholics, who felt that the spirit of freedom that inspired Vatican II had disappeared and the fire of renewal in the local Church was extinguished. Schillebeeckx's conclusion was that, given this ecclesial malfunctioning, it was not really worthwhile to reflect theologically on the Church at that moment. Psychologically understandable as this response may be, as a theological statement it is shocking. As if 'the Church' is restricted to the practice of a group of ecclesiastics and their discourse, as if ecclesiology comes down to legitimizing current ecclesiological practices, and as if one of the main ecclesiological questions has not always been whether, how, and in what sense a far from perfect, malfunctioning, and sinful Church can mediate God's salvation!

IV The Church as sacrament

The common criticism of Vatican II has become that it was too optimistic about the modern world. In the light of the worldwide impact of the sexual abuse crisis, I would argue, however, that a much graver problem is its optimism about the Church. There has been a strong tendency in ecclesiology in the twentieth century, both in 'conservative' and 'progressive' circles, to see the Church as the exception that can save the rest of the world from evil and sin. This did not change at the Council. The fact that the Church is just as bad as the rest of the world, however, becomes rather obvious time and again.

Karl Rahner was a notable exception when he wrote in a still remarkable article from as early as 1947, with all due clarity: 'the Church is sinful'. If sinners do not lose their Church membership through their sinfulness, as is Catholic teaching, and if the Church is a real existing body whose members are actual persons, not some general idea or vague ideal, we can only conclude that the Church in itself is sinful. This implies, according to Rahner, that Church leaders are sinful and are leading the Church not only through their connection with the Holy Spirit but also according to their sinfulness. This sinful Church led by sinners is ultimately holy, in Rahner's view, not from what it is or owns – neither from its institution by Christ himself, nor from the legacy of the words and deeds of the historical Jesus – but from its openness to the reception of God's presence to it through the infallible divine faithfulness of the God in Jesus Christ through the Spirit. And in parentheses Rahner scribbled what might be the most important sentence of the whole essay: 'How far from self-evident is this miracle of the power and the grace of [its] Holy Spirit; yet it is ever renewed through the centuries'.[17]

Schillebeeckx sometimes comes close to this. Toward the end of

Church the Human Story of God, Schillebeeckx wrote that no one and nothing outside or inside the Church holds a lease on the Spirit of God. All are dependent on and are put into perspective by 'the living God, who brings his creation in Jesus Christ, through our history, to a final consummation after history'.[18] This is not about a Church that threatens to extinguish the Spirit, but about a Spirit that keeps the Church dynamic and inspires it to an existence in relation to the world and its history that are understood as the spaces of God's presence. This ultimately implies that the Church has not just been initiated within history by Jesus but that also, time and again, it has been, is being, and will be opened up and appealed to by the Anointed One and his Spirit to render its services to the approaching Kingdom of God. To put it somewhat differently, the radical reinterpretation and re-creation in the light of God's close future, the sundering of set conditions, was typical of Jesus' actions. If he is forever the Living One since the resurrection and the ascension, he remains active among us, breaking open and recreating, rather than coinciding with the Church as it has become or with the inherited memory of his actions and his message.

The retrieval of this ongoing, renewing presence of the living Christ seems to have been what Schillebeeckx was ultimately striving for. In 1983, in his valedictory speech as a professor at Nijmegen University, Schillebeeckx introduced the idea of what he called a 'proportional identity' between Jesus and the message present in the words and deeds of contemporary believers: the message contemporary people embody by following Jesus should relate to their situation in the same way as Jesus' message and actions were related to his situation.[19] Loyalty to Jesus' message is not preaching the same substantial message, but participating and intervening in the contemporary context in the same way as Jesus participated and intervened in his context. This is a rather revolutionary idea, because it introduces the current social-cultural context into the very core of revelation itself. It is no longer a revelation in the past that needs to be reinterpreted time and again in order to have some meaning for the present. The revelatory aspect of Jesus Christ's life, death, and resurrection continually needs to be discovered within ever-changing historical contexts.

Speaking of proportional identity ultimately signifies that the foundation of the continuity within the Christian Church is neither one-sidedly Jesus as he still speaks to contemporary people and inspires them from his history, as Schillebeeckx often suggests, nor is it found in the hierarchical Church and the apostolic succession. The continuity is ultimately theological and lies hidden in the Christ who lives within God and still manifests himself through the Holy Spirit to the world. The Christ who makes his presence felt in the Spirit is not simply an object of faith and theology from the past or in the Church's witness, but the source of an ever-unexpected dynamic that cannot be anticipated. Truly witnessing to Jesus Christ in faith is forever new and renewing, and he himself is the one that makes this possible time and again. The Church, in this way of thinking, is not the guarantee or the embodiment of the presence of God in history. The Church is called to bear *witness* to the fact that 'Christ is the Light of nations', as the opening paragraph of *Lumen Gentium* puts it. So it is 'a sacrament'. It does not *own* this sacramentality, but the Church is constantly *made* a sacrament by the faithful, enduring, and ever coming presence of the triune God.

V Sacramentalizing human history

This brings us back, finally, to Schillebeeckx's article on the necessity and the possibility of rediscovering the meaning of the sacraments though the input of Ritual Studies. What fascinated Schillebeeckx, clearly, was the way Ritual Studies reversed the traditional order in thinking about sacramental signs in the theological tradition. Theologically the emphasis has always been on that what the ritual mediates to the world: meaning, a message, a presence even. Ritual Studies concentrate on what rituals capture, unite, bring together in a meaningful manner from ordinary life. The classical question is, so to say, how the living Christ is present in the host. Ritual Studies stress the fact that Christ's presence is celebrated in bread and what that fact signifies. For Schillebeeckx, this resonates with the incarnation. In Jesus, God was not in the world as a stranger, but 'he came unto his own', as the prologue of the Gospel of John phrases it, and enabled everything to 'return to its own', to retrieve its place in God's plan, which is the foundation of creation. Sacraments are not telling the world what it should be and how it should be different, but are revealing what the world truly is and what our lives as human beings truly are, and how we therefore can and should act. Just as Jesus Christ was not divine because he was less human, but because he was truly human, bread is not the body of Christ by being less 'breadly', but by becoming truly and fully bread: life-giving food that creates community.

This sets a new agenda, not simply for future reflections on the sacraments, but for theology as such. Its ultimate goal is not to mediate a divine message to a godless contemporary world, but to show how this contemporary world is the space for the nearness of God's reign. Theology's task is to show how history is sacramental, how it is sign and instrument of the presence of the God Jesus preached. As Vatican II stressed in the Pastoral Consitution on the Church in the Modern World *Gaudium et Spes*: 'The People of God believes that it is led by the Spirit of the Lord who fills the whole world. Impelled by that faith, it tries to discern the true signs of God's presence and purpose in the events, the needs and the desires which it shares with the rewst of humanity today' (no. 11).

This, I would argue, should be the focus for a theology that seeks to be both truly theological and truly contemporary. How is God our God? What does that mean for our understanding of the world, our behaviour, our building of a society and a Church, our celebration of life as a presence of what is coming and an anticipation of what reveals itself as anticipation? The Church revolves around the sacraments because ultimately it believes and celebrates that God is sacramentally present, like Jesus, 'among us' (cf. Luke 17.21).

Notes

1. E. Schillebeeckx, *De sacramentele heilseconomie. Theologische bezinning op S. Thomas' sacramentenleer in het licht van de traditie en van de hedendaagse sacramentsproblematiek*, I, Antwerp: 't Groeit; Bilthoven: Nelissen, 1952.
2. For the background to Schillebeeckx's book on the sacraments, cf. my *Edward Schillebeeckx: A Theologian in His History*, Part I: *A Catholic Theology of Culture (1914–1965),* London & New York: Continuum, 2003, pp. 199–216.
3. E. Schillebeeckx, 'Naar een herontdekking van de christelijke sacramenten: Ritualisering van religieuze momenten in het alledaagse leven', *Tijdschrift voor Theologie* 40 (2000), pp. 164–87; partly translated as 'Towards a Rediscovery of the Christian Sacraments: Ritualizing Religious Elements in Daily Life', in: D. G. Lange and D. W. Vogel (eds), *Ordo: Bath, Word, Prayer, Table,* Akron: OSL Publications, 2005, pp. 6–34. See also E. Schillebeeckx, *Theologisch testament: Notarieel nog niet verleden,* Baarn: Nelissen, 1994, pp. 185–91, 'Verzet en inzet, overgave en viering'.
4. Schillebeeckx, *De sacramentele heilseconomie,* p. 142.
5. E. Schillebeeckx, *Christus sacrament van de Godsontmoeting,* Bilthoven: Nelissen 1959; Eng. trans. *Christ the Sacrament of the Encounter with God,* New York: Sheed & Ward, 1963.

6. See E. Schillebeeckx, *Jesus an Experiment in Christology,* New York: Crossroad, 1979, p. 52.
7. *Ibid.,* pp. 64–76.
8. *Ibid.*, p. 650.
9. *Ibid.,* p. 61.
10. Cf. R. Bultmann, *Neues Testament und Mythologie: Das Problem der Entmythologisierung der neutestamentlichen Verkündigung,* Munich: Kaiser, 1985 (original 1941).
11. Cf. W. Kasper & J. Moltmann, *Jesus ja – Kirche nein?,* Zürich: Benzinger Verlag, 1973.
12. Schillebeeckx, *Jesus,* p. 649; cf. his earlier comments on Jesus' resurrection on pp. 329–98. For the debate on Schillebeeckx's views on the resurrection, see E. Schillebeeckx, *Interim Report on the Books* Jesus *and* Christ*,* London: SCM Press, 1980, pp. 74–93; for the confrontation on this with the Congregation for the Doctrine of Faith, see T. Schoof (ed.), *The Schillebeeckx Case: Official Exchange of Letters and Documents,* New York: Ramsey, 1984.
13. E. Schillebeeckx, *Christ the Experience of Jesus as Lord,* New York: The Seabury Press, 1980, pp. 641–2.
14. Schillebeeckx, *Jesus*, p. 379.
15. For further explanation of the idea that Jesus' message, oriented toward a future in God, continues after his death and, guided by the Spirit, finds new and previously unseen forms, entirely in tune with the future-oriented character, see my book *Wortelen in vaste grond: Een cultuurtheologisch essay,* Zoetermeer, 2009. It is my intention systematically to develop this view on the work of the Spirit, and its consequences for theology in the coming years.
16· Cf. esp. E. Schillebeeckx, *The Understanding of Faith: Interpretation and Criticism*, London: Sheed and Ward, 1974, where he protests against an interpretation of Christian faith that is too one-sidedly oriented toward contemporary relevance. See also the title of his *God the Future of Man,* New York & London: Sheed and Ward, 1968, which partly reprints the same articles.
17. E. Schillebeeckx, *Church the Human Story of God,* New York: Crossroad, 1990, p. xiii.
18. K. Rahner, *Schriften zur Theologie* VI: *Neuere Schriften,* Einsiedeln/Zürich/Köln: Benzinger Verlag, 1965, pp. 301–20: 'Kirche der Sünder' (1947). Eng. trans. In *A Rahner Reader,* ed. Gerald A. McCool, New York: Crossroad, 1981, pp. 300–5.
19. Schillebeeckx, *Church,* p. 228.
20. E. Schillebeeckx, *Theologisch geloofsverstaan anno 1983,* Baarn: Nelissen, 1983, pp. 14–17; Schillebeeckx, *Church the Human Story of God*, pp. 40–5. The idea matches that of C. Boff in his *Theology and Praxis: Epistemological Foundations*, Maryknoll: Orbis Books, 1987 (revised edition), pp. 146–50.

The Eucharist: Remembrance, Anticipation, Real Presence

JENNIFER COOPER

The Eucharist is 'the source and the summit of the Christian life' (*Lumen Gentium* 11). It is very fitting that a reflection on the Eucharist is included in this edition in honour of Edward Schillebeeckx, who himself described the Eucharist as the 'distinctive density of Christ's real presence', the event giving expression to 'the deepest meaning of (our) continuing history'.[1] He contributed substantively to the reception and interpretation of the spirit of the Second Vatican Council in its liturgical renewal and the renewal of eucharistic theology, mindful always that eucharistic theology in every age is an unceasing interpretation of Christ's personal presence in our midst.[2] And as we approach 50 years since the convening of the first session of the Council, his own theology of the Eucharist remains a rich resource for the Church, perhaps most especially within the English-speaking world, where the recent revisions of the liturgy have once again called Catholics to a renewed reflection on the eucharistic mystery in and through its liturgical expression.

Edward Schillebeeckx was a theologian of the encounter between God and humanity. His work over so many years was a continuous and ever-new reflection on this reality. His theology is characterized by confidence in 'God's personal presence [as] always the deepest relationship *in everything*'.[3] His great theological mentor Marie-Dominique Chenu would describe Schillebeeckx's theology as 'audacious', something he would well have recognized in Schillebeeckx, for Schillebeeckx himself learnt much from Chenu and his school of theology.[4]

Schillebeeckx described the sacraments as 'interpersonal encounters' between God and humanity. It is perhaps unsurprising then that his theological writings begin and end with sacramental theology.[5] His first book was *De Sacramentele Heilseconomie* – the sacramental economy of salvation.[6] And an unfinished work written towards the end of his life returned again to the theme of sacramental theology. A glimpse of this work was given in an article entitled 'Toward a Rediscovery of the Christian Sacraments'.[7] His one monograph dedicated specifically to eucharistic theology, *The Eucharist,* is slim, and he confessed toward the end of it: 'I have struggled with the interpretation of this *mysterium fidei*'. Yet his eucharistic theology has been greatly influential both for Catholic theology and more widely, as it has fostered a good deal of ecumenical discussion. Its enduring influence lies in what he described as its realism: 'God himself acts in the sphere of the actively believing, doing and celebrating Church, and the result of this divine saving activity is sacramentally a "new creation" which perpetuates and deepens our eschatological relationship to the kingdom of God'.[8] The Eucharist is that interpersonal encounter between God and humanity that gives the deepest meaning to our human lives.

Schillebeeckx's little book on the Eucharist is now dated in one particular respect. The prevailing trend in post-Vatican II theology has been to interpret eucharistic theology from within the liturgy, from within the actions and words of the liturgy of the Eucharist itself. There have been numerous studies that focus on the Eucharistic Prayers in particular as sources for theology of the Eucharist. And there are other studies that consider the whole of the liturgy as a source for theology – one notable example is *Models of the Eucharist* by Kevin Irwin.[9] Irwin reminds us of the classical adage attributed to Prosper of Aquitaine: 'the rule of prayer establishes the rule of belief'.[10] The liturgical texts and rites themselves are primary sources for theology. This only serves to underscore how significant the renewal of liturgy is, for there is 'no such thing as "just" a liturgical change. Among other things, to change a rite is at once to change or to adjust our notions of God, of ourselves, of each other, of grace, of redemption, of the church etc.'[11]

In the years since the Council, the renewed liturgies and rites of the Church have proved rich resources for a renewed sacramental theology. The reception of the council documents on liturgy, along with the liturgical rites and texts, has been ongoing, generating a fruitful environment for theological reflection on the meaning of the sacraments, not least the Eucharist. This reflection has not been limited to liturgical theologians. In the ongoing interpretation of the spirit of the Council with respect to liturgy and the sacraments, there has been a renewed interest in the contributions of those theologians whose work in the years prior to the Council itself paved the way for the theology and liturgy that emerged in its wake. A new collection in translation of liturgical essays written by Yves Congar is a sign of this interest.[12] The recent translation of Henri de Lubac's *Corpus Mysticum*, is another.[13] And the theology of Marie-Dominique Chenu has received greater attention. His theology, although not as well known in the English-speaking world as that of some of his contemporaries, offers, in its very structure and method, an invaluable resource for eucharistic theology.

Congar once described the incarnation as the general principle and dynamic governing Chenu's theology.[14] This theme has been taken up and developed by Christophe Potworowski in *Contemplation and Incarnation: The Theology of Marie-Dominique Chenu*.[15] Chenu's own discussion of the structure and dynamism of theology is found in his essay on the Saulchoir.[16] Here we find a vision of theology built upon Chenu's confidence in the presence and activity of the Word in human history. Theology is given as gift in God's self-revelation. The task of theology is to make the Word incarnate in human words. The life of faith is participation in God's self-knowledge. Faith is not self-generating; it is dependent upon the Word, the gift of God's speaking.[17] Faith is both a gracious divine activity – it is given as gift – and also a fully human activity – faith is received in human reason.[18]

It is here in this incarnational understanding of the relation between faith and reason that the dynamism and structure of Chenu's own theology is found. What is most significant is the insight that the incarnation does not provide simply a model for understanding or explaining the relation of faith to reason. It is not simply an illustration. Faith is to reason what the divine is to the human in the mystery of the incarnation in an analogous manner. Faith is not the remembrance of things past, it is the activity of the living Word present and active in human reason. Faith is that activity that makes us *contemporains du Christ*.[19] This is what Chenu means when he describes theology as 'audacious': theology is the *science des enfants de Dieu*.[20]

Congar drew attention to the incarnational structure of Chenu's theology. At its heart lies a profoundly incarnational realism. Faith becomes incarnate in reason. Faith does not simply illuminate reason.

Just as the Word is not diminished in becoming flesh so too faith is not diminished by becoming enfleshed in reason.[21] The relation of faith to reason participates in the christological mystery in which the divine and the human are one. The context for this particular working out of the relationship between reason and faith and hence for the approach to theology, as Congar noted, was Chenu's interpretation of the nature-grace relation. Grace becomes incarnate in nature, and so too faith becomes incarnate in reason. Faith is therefore a divine gift and a fully human reality. If we know God, we know God humanly.[22]

For Chenu, theology has an incarnational structure that participates in the divine-human relation revealed in the christological mystery. Yet, he recognized a paradox at the heart of all of this. The Word present and active in history gives rise to a paradox – revelation is accomplished only in its reception. The Word is given to us *in* human words. The infinite and transcendent, the mystery of God's self-gift, becomes incarnate and known within the limits – the finitude – of human reality. Chenu called this the paradox of faith.[23] This paradox itself yields very rich dividends for theology. Theology is by its very dynamism and structure engaged with the human. Theology is not the mere repetition of tradition. It is by its very nature engaged with human history – it is a constant exploration and re-exploration of tradition in response to the questions and pastoral needs of its context and time. Theology cannot be abstracted from history.[24] Rather, theology must seek to understand and express the transcendent mystery of God revealed in the historical events of God.

Chenu's incarnational method offers much to sacramental theology, and this finds its most acute expression in his theology of the Eucharist. Here perhaps Chenu's paradox of faith becomes especially concentrated, for what is given to us in the Eucharist is the giver himself. Schillebeeckx expresses the incarnational paradox of the Eucharist thus:

> "This is my body, this is my blood": this is not a giving of oneself in a gift, not even at a more profound level because the giver here is Christ, the personal revelation of the Father. No, what is given to us in the Eucharist is nothing other than Christ himself. What the sacramental forms of bread and wine signify, and at the same time make real, is not a gift that refers to Christ who gives himself in them, but Christ himself in living personal presence.[25]

Schillebeeckx inherited from Chenu the conviction that the mystery of God is revealed in historical events of God – and his little book on the Eucharist opens with a reflection on the truth that 'grace makes history'.[26] For Schillebeeckx, as for Chenu, faith is both a divine gift and a human activity. Struggling to interpret transubstantiation and transignification, and the relation between these, he offered an explanation that sounded very like Chenu's incarnational realism: God acts within the human activity of giving meaning. 'I can never rest content with an appeal to a human giving meaning alone . . . [O]f course, a transignification of this kind has taken place in the Eucharist, but it is borne up and evoked by the re-creative activity of the Holy Spirit, the Spirit of Christ sent by the Father. God himself acts in the sphere of the actively believing, doing and celebrating Church.' And then he goes on: '[A]nd the result of this divine saving activity is sacramentally a "new creation" which perpetuates and deepens our eschatological relationship to the kingdom of God'.[27] Here something that remained implicit in Chenu, the relation between the incarnational and the eschatological, becomes explicit with Schillebeeckx.

The relation between history and eschatology runs as a theme throughout the whole of Schillebeeckx's theology. It is brought into particularly sharp focus in his theology of the Eucharist as he reflects on the relation between anamnesis and our encounter now with the risen Christ in the enactment of the Eucharist. 'Our personal relationship with the Lord is also essentially an anamnesis, a calling to mind of the historical event of salvation on the cross, not insofar as it is past, but insofar as it endures eternally in its completion. The eternity is however, not situated behind history, but accomplished in history'.[28] The sacramental is the making visible and present in the midst of our human history a fully eschatological mystery.

In a revealing phrase, Schillebeeckx himself acknowledges his particular interpretation of the relation between history and eschatology and its significance for his eucharistic theology. In the midst of his discussion of 'real presence', he interposes: 'I should like to place much greater emphasis than most modern authors have done on this essential bond between the real presence of Christ in the Eucharist and his real presence as Lord living in the Church'.[29] Our eucharistic anamnesis is of the living Lord of history – of the Lord who died but is living.[30] In our present in our eucharistic act of remembering, we encounter the eschatological promise and fulfilment of our human lives, for 'Christ is present in the Eucharist as the Lord – that is as the one who gave himself in death "for our sins" and was brought to life for us by God'.[31]

Schillebeeckx did not undertake a liturgical study of the Eucharist. He worried that to do so would transform one slight volume into a trilogy – a concern rooted in experience. Yet even if his book on the Eucharist cannot be described as liturgical theology, he certainly recognized the significance of the enactment of liturgy as the primary source for a eucharistic theology. In his introduction to *The Eucharist*, he acknowledged that a discussion of transubstantiation can really only be undertaken fully within 'the whole context of the liturgical sacramental event'.[32] This conviction that the Eucharist is an event and its interpretation can be found only in the enactment of this event is borne out in the whole of Schillebeeckx's eucharistic theology. And because this is the case, it is still a rich resource now at a time in Catholic life and thought when reflection on the Eucharist and liturgical renewal remains of pressing significance.

Lumen Gentium described the Eucharist as the source and the summit of Christian life. Schillebeeckx described it as sufficient for Christian life.

> The living Christ identifies himself with the community at table, he himself becomes the food and drink that is offered at the meal, and we can live in this community from his redeeming death and his being raised to power by the Father. This is sufficient for Christian life.[33]

Notes

1. Edward Schillebeeckx, *The Eucharist*, London: Sheed and Ward, 1968, pp. 103; 124.
2. *Ibid.*, p. 92.
3. *Ibid.*, p. 129.
4. Marie-Dominique Chenu, *Une école de théologie: le Saulchoir*, Paris: Les Éditions du Cerf, 1985, p. 150.
5. Schillebeeckx, *The Eucharist*, p. 101. Sacrament as interpersonal encounter between God and humanity is the theme of his *Christ the Sacrament of the Encounter with God*, London: Sheed and Ward, 1963.
6. E. Schillebeeckx, *De Sacramentele Heilseconomie*. This has relatively recently been translated as *L'économie sacramentelle du salut*, Fribourg: Academic Press, 2004). This is a very welcome addition as Schillebeeckx's approach to sacramental theology has significant promise for future developments.

7. Schillebeeckx, 'Naar een herontdekking van de chistelijke sacramenten', *Tijdschrift voor Theologie* 40 (2000), pp. 164–87.
8. Schillebeeckx, *The Eucharist*, p. 151.
9. Kevin Irwin, *Models of the Eucharist*, Mahwah, NJ: Paulist Press, 2005.
10. As cited by Irwin, *Models of the Eucharist*, p. 25; p. 334 n. 6.
11. *Ibid.*, p. 26.
12. *At the Heart of Christian Worship. Liturgical Essays of Yves Congar*, trans. and ed. Paul Philibert, Collegeville, MN: Liturgical Press, 2010.
13. Henri de Lubac, *Corpus Mysticum*, trans. Gemma Simmonds, Notre Dame, IN: University of Notre Dame Press and London: SCM Press, 2006.
14. Congar, 'Le Père Chenu', in *Bilan de la théologie du XXe siècle*, II, ed. Robert Vander Grucht and Herbert Vorgrimler, pp. 772–90 (here 781).
15. Christophe Potoworowski, *Contemplation and Incarnation: The Theology of Marie-Dominique Chenu*, Montreal: McGill-Queen's University Press, 2001.
16. Chenu, *Une école de théologie.*
17. *Ibid.*, pp. 134–6.
18. Congar, 'Le Père Chenu', p. 780.
19. Chenu, *Une école de théologie*, pp. 135–6.
20. *Ibid.* p. 150.
21. *Ibid*, p. 137. 'Pas plus que la grâce en la nature, la foi n'est une lumière posée à la surface d'une raison: elle vit en elle. Et la foi n'est pas contaminée par cette incarnation, pas plus que le Verbe n'est amoindri pour s'être fait chair. Double mystère théandrique, mieux, unique mystère même du Christ, en qui le divin et l'humain sont un: unique Personne, en laquelle la foi me plante, Fils éternel de Dieu entré dans l'histoire.'
22. *Ibid.*, p. 137. 'Si vraiment l'homme connaît Dieu, il le connaîtra humainement.'
23. *Ibid.*, pp. 136; 138. 'Paradoxe de la foi . . . La parole de Dieu est *dans* la parole humaine: la force de Dieu se révèle dans cette infirmité.'
24. See the Preface written by Chenu to Claude Geffré, *Un nouvel âge de la théologie*, Paris: Les Éditions du Cerf, 1987, pp. 7–10.
25. Schillebeeckx, *The Eucharist*, p. 139.
26. *Ibid.*, p. 19.
27. *Ibid.*, p. 151.
28. *Ibid.*, p. 126.
29. *Ibid.,* p. 136.
30. *Ibid.*, p. 136.
31. *Ibid.*, p.126.
32. *Ibid.*, p. 19.
33. *Ibid.*, p. 125.

The Sacraments: Real Event vs Empty Symbolism or Occult Magic

ANDRÉS TORRES QUEIRUGA

The sacraments have been a major topic of discussion throughout Christian history. In the context of Vatican II – both before and after – study of them intensified, with a recovery of tradition and a search for new possibilities. This was not accidental: cultural change has been so marked that a large part of traditional expression has become simply meaningless and in need of significant reformulation. This is no easy task, since the accumulated wealth surrounding them has become so vast that, as Karl Rahner said and Eberhard Jüngel recalled, 'saying something significant' was likely to be reduced to 'a couple of arbitrarily chosen contributions', without amounting to a 'rounded and well-supported response'.[1]

The task, then, is as necessary as it is humble. My only purpose here is to approach the basic meaning of the sacraments, paying particular attention to the deformations that impede their understanding in a firmly secular society. These deformations may have been superseded on the *theoretical* level, but as they are mediated through the same old *vocabulary* and enshrined in some liturgical *practices*, they still distort the common perception and contaminate many theological presuppositions. So I am seeking not to contribute new data to the current wealth of research, but to propose a point of view that may help to reconfigure and bring together widespread anxieties and questions in such a way that, without losing the reality of the sacraments in an actually empty symbolism or an occultly magical approach, may provide a meaningful vision for *now*.[2]

I From anthropology to theology

I was planning this article at the time of the horrible assassinations in

Oslo – an event beyond comprehension, a terrifying threat that seemed to break all bounds of meaning. But people did not run away or keep silent: they reacted by coming together, in intimate and solemn actions, with candles, flowers, words, and song. When the Norwegian writer Jostein Gaarder was asked about it, he said: 'Hundreds of thousands of Norwegians are showing their sorrow with flowers in their hands; there is a mutual promise being made at this time: we suffer together, we share the pain. We respond to hate and agony with hope.'[3] Perhaps not all were conscious of the significance, but they 'lived' it. As Blondel knew, we often carry out what we do not fully understand.

This event was exceptional, but it illustrates an anthropological constant: expressing ourselves through actions and rituals, individual or communal, such as holding up white-painted hands to demand peace, or saying thank-you with a gift – 'Say it with flowers'. Salient events prove particularly significant because, by stirring the roots of our being and of meaning, they break the surface and invite us – or can invite us – to go farther and transcend our empirical existence.

In Oslo, in fact, the lights in the square were mirrored in church ceremonies. And many people certainly took part in both demonstrations, which shows a basic *continuum* of meaning between the secular and the religious spheres. Believers share in the general experience: they differ basically only in (their conviction of) *also* discovering that we are not alone in the endeavour to re-build meaning and keep hoping, but that we are joined and protected by God as founding Transcendence. Peter Berger, looking for human actions in which this Transcendence can show through, gives the good example of a child waking up and being afraid of the dark. Its mother calms it by saying, 'Don't be afraid. Everything is in order, everything is all right.' To the obvious question, 'Is the mother lying to her child?', he replies that the answer 'can be "No" only if there is some truth in the religious interpretation of human existence', since God alone can guarantee this truth, as all mothers perhaps dimly grasp.[4]

The religious foundation does not eliminate the primary meaning; it enriches it, since it accepts it in its integrity and *furthermore* shows it in its deep and ultimate truth. The sacraments fall into this sphere. On the one hand, they do not deny the secular significance but 'unveil what is hidden to the world while, at the same time, deciding about the world'.[5] On the other hand, they keep the 'family atmosphere' they share with the rites of other religions, opening them up to dialogue, which is so important and enriching today.

This provides the real setting for a truly meaningful updating. As they have been handed down in their (late-)medieval formulation, the sacraments seem laden with a strong dose of objectivism, as 'things' that 'contain' grace (as in a 'vessel', as Hugh of St Victor wrote; cf. Trent: DS 1606), and as physical 'instruments' that, through a sort of 'invisible miracle', produce 'invisible' effects through their own dynamism (*ex opere operato*). The common understanding of infant Baptism provides a terribly effective example of this. In today's general understanding, the sacraments thereby come to represent an occult and unbelievable magic, which, by reaction, can lead to an outward symbolism of equally incredible empty rites. Allied to this is a juridicism that often converts what is essentially a gift and a present into an obligation and even a heavy burden: 'obligation' to go to confession in order to receive infinitely *gratuitous* forgiveness, Sunday 'duty' to *enjoy* the Lord's Banquet.

We can now see that the problem consists not only, or even mainly, in upholding the *fact* of the saving Presence, but in clarifying *how* it comes about, in such a way as to reflect both the infinite gratuitousness of the God-of-Jesus and free human responsibility. It would be deeply unfair to reduce tradition to its defects, since reality is always richer than theory. But it would be equally foolhardy not to undertake its revision, since only by making it relevant for today will it be possible to discover and enjoy its riches. Two crucial moments signpost the way: the Reformation and Modernity.

II The Reformation and Modernity as crisis and opportunity

The Reformation summed up a new religious unease, with its stress on the subjective dimension. Its '*sola scriptura*', requiring the life of Jesus to be taken as legitimation and model, promoted concentration on the essential: 'The Holy Scriptures have only one sacrament, which is Christ himself, the Lord'.[6] '*Sola fide*' forced a revision of the deformations brought about by the (misunderstood) *operatum*,[7] insisting on the importance of the Word, inward participation by the heart, and the exclusion of the commercialism of 'merit'. Trent itself took up the challenge, introducing greater conceptual flexibility and pastoral regeneration. Nevertheless, it stressed – in a one-sided counter-reaction – the objectivity of signs, while polemically upholding traditional vocabulary and concepts.

Modernity, however, provided the greater challenge, reaching as it did to the roots and shaking the foundations. From a historical perspective, many of the inter-confessional controversies – among the Reformed Churches too – now look like family quarrels, involving differences that often seem irrelevant. Christologically, biblical criticism made it impossible to sustain a literal 'institution' of the sacraments,[8] while theologically, the affirmation of worldly autonomy de-legitimized any interventionist conception of divine action, requiring a fundamental re-thinking of sacramental causality. It was a real paradigm shift.

There was a significant time-lapse before the Churches rose to the challenge, and confessional disputes made this even harder. But sacramental theology has begun the process and made some major advances, thanks partly to the use it has made of human sciences such as history, the phenomenology of religion, linguistic pragmatism, and the philosophy of symbolical forms, and partly by concentrating on essentials. In the Catholic field, the initiatives of Rahner and Schillebeeckx, basing their reflection on the *Church* as 'foundational sacrament' and on *Christ* as 'originating sacrament', have been especially fruitful. This has brought about a break from scholastic rigidities, in a full re-reading of the Tradition, paying attention to both the mysteries of the life of Christ and the great suggestive wealth of Church liturgy, including that of the Eastern Churches. Numerous liturgical and theological initiatives are trying to move beyond outmoded concepts and to reveal the intellectual meaningfulness of the sacraments and the way they are rooted in real life.

We have not yet, however, achieved a single overall vision capable of embodying all our over-dispersed and heterogeneous accumulations, often based on culturally outdated presuppositions. We need to find a central signifier that, taking the new data as a sort of phenomenological 'variations', might reveal an 'essence' capable of articulating them in an ongoing actualized understanding – postulated by Mircea Eliade for any understanding of religious phenomena. There is still clearly a long way to go, but if we take account of the two main considerations I have pointed out – biblical renewal and modern revolution – it seems possible to indicate the correct route.

III Interpreting God's action in the new culture

Despite reservations and inevitable disagreements, we can state that – as express acceptance or irreversible ferment – the findings of biblical criticism have now become part of current theology. What is needed now is to complement them with an account of the resulting impact of Modernity on human freedom and how we see God at work.

Sacramental theology was forged within a cosmovision that took continual divine intervention for granted. Natural substances, such as holy water, or various formulas and ceremonies were seen as spontaneously causing both spiritual and empirical effects – increasing grace, healing bodies, or bringing rain. This cosmovision has vanished beyond recall. Even where practices or routines that seem to contradict this remain, they are 'remnants' in full retreat within the Churches, and outside these look like anachronisms that make religion unbelievable. We have fortunately made progress, but the fancies linger: anointing forgives sins, but can also restore physical health; Christ is always with us but 'comes down' at the consecration in the Eucharist. The same goes for certain practices such as absolving or anointing an unconscious or even dead person, or in some still usual interpretations of infant Baptism. The worst of this is that this vision shapes the '*schema*' of people's imagination, making them see the sacraments of 'instruments' of a particular divine action initiated by their celebration.

This account is cruelly schematic, but by showing the structure, it shows that detailed changes will not do. The various components of this view all hold together, forming a network deeply embedded in religious and theological imaginings. Only by fashioning a remodelling of the whole will it be possible to achieve a new coherence that can make sacraments understandable, credible, and acceptable in the new cultural situation.

Theology is in fact faced with a dilemma: it cannot interpret the efficacy of the sacraments as special divine 'interventionism' without drifting into magic; but without real efficacy the sacraments would be reduced to empty symbolism or mere acting 'as if'. If we cannot achieve clarity on this point, the progress made in sacramental theology cannot become fully coherent. Fortunately, just as happened with biblical criticism, if we do not succumb to bewilderment, to fundamentalist repetition, or to superficial adaptation, the new situation can bring a fresh possibility along with the problem.

IV Retaking tradition and understanding 'from below'

This possibility arises precisely from two fundamental truths of tradition: *continuous creation* and God as *already ever-given love*.[9] These turn everything around, enabling an understanding that, within losing any traditional gains, can prove capable of being brought cleanly and fruitfully into the present. They break radically with the dualist scenario that Barth brusquely handed out with theological passion but potentially disastrous results: 'God is in heaven, and you're on earth'.[10] A god 'there' and us 'here' *imaginatively* implies that he has to 'decide' to act through 'instruments', on particular occasions. Barth is overstating his case: he found it difficult to understand sacraments, to the extent that L.-M. Chauvet analysed 'the non-sacramentality of Barth',[11] and Bonhoeffer criticized his excessive 'actualism'. But the scenario is broader than Barth: almost without exception, manuals – even 'renewed' ones – start 'from above', making sacraments *precise* [occasional, isolated???] actions by God through Christ and the Church.

Clearly, we are not concerned with denying the essential truth of this view, but we do have to alter its viewpoint. If God is *pure act* and absolute initiative, if God is *love* 'still working' (John 5.17) for our salvation, in 'loving contention' with our resistance and passivity, then the change *is not in God, but in ourselves*: it is we and not God who need to begin again and to change. God's initiative is permanent and sure; it is only our *response* that is unsure: 'Listen! I am standing at the door, knocking. If you hear my voice and open the door, I will come in to you [. . .]' (Rev. 3.20). The sacraments should focus on providing our response.

Stating this does not deny the *reality* of divine action, reducing it to an 'as if'. But it is just in human acceptance that transcendent action – real, faithful, unfailing – becomes grace *happening* and historical *newness*. God is *already* loving the wounded and calling the neighbour, but it is only when the Samaritan hears the call that effective salvation comes about, in him and in the wounded man.

This applies to any valid form of religious life, and also to the sacraments, which are exceptional ways of experiencing it and bringing it about. This is why we need to approach them 'from below' – devising community events that, through symbols, rites, and words create a celebratory space that helps to *hear and effectively accept* the call, transforming the already-and-always-granted *Presence* into actually saving *encounter*. All its elements – recollection, demonstration, prognosis (cf. STh 3,60,4) – are designed to strengthen faith, foment love, and sustain hope, taking as their ultimate model the life of Christ as the definitive revelation of God's love. And they all exist and happen thanks to the absolute initiative that founds them and calls them forth: 'No one can come to me unless drawn by the Father' (John 6.44).

This approach 'from below' does not break with tradition or contribute anything especially new; still less does it claim to be an exclusive viewpoint. It does, though, allow a re-reading that sheds light – sometimes in surprising ways – on the wealth of tradition through a real cultural tuning. It thereby opens up a journey that, in my view, can prove extraordinarily fruitful. On the way, many points that seemed thorny resolve themselves, and the practical consequences of sacramental realism become more apparent.

V Toward an updated understanding

Such an understanding will in the first place take in the *fact* of the sacraments. On the one hand, they can be seen to be deeply rooted in the *human symbolic system*, free of any impression of being an *ad hoc* construction or a supernaturalist intrusion into the legitimate autonomy of the world or human freedom. On the other, they reflect the *dynamic of the incarnation*, so essentially Christian, which shows them as particular examples of a general sacramentality that has its originating nuclei in the corporeality of Christ and the community of the Church. This gives rise to the existence of 'sacramentals' or the importance of celebrations and, in a general sense, to the possibility of a 'diaphany' (Teilhard de Chardin) that views everything in life and the world as sacramental manifestation.

This understanding also clarifies the *specificity* of the sacraments. God's saving presence is always active, fully and really, in *all* situations. But human life is variable and polyphonic, so the manner of the divine presence is necessarily varied. The sacraments apply to 'limit-situations' (Jaspers), in which we need this presence more acutely. Different situations specify each sacrament: birth, death, change of life . . ., with, embracing them all, the Eucharist as central celebration in which, 'in the mystery of the Word made flesh', the ever threatened and fragile overall meaning of existence – ultimate limit – is revealed and proclaimed (GS 22).

The *number seven* also becomes clear with no great difficulty. In effect, theology has always *also* dealt with life situations.[12] But the 'from above' approach got in the way: no clear 'deduction' could be made from Christ or the Church. Approached from below, the number seven appears realistic and flexible: church instinct – rather than defined theory – placed the sacraments in limit-situations. Experience indicated them, and reference to Jesus marked the style without dictating the detail. Rahner elucidated that by working in this way the Church was proceeding with 'divine right': in clarifying the Founder's intention, it configured the symbols and upheld the *factual* legitimacy of the seven: '*nec plura nec pauciora*'.

This implies that the Church enjoys a certain freedom in making this *historical decision* – a freedom that, rooted in life and in solidarity with human religious history, could, for instance, clarify the place of *Confirmation*, so muddled by its history (and perhaps by over-literal interpretation). Everything points to its place as a rite of passage marking the end of adolescence, in which the Spirit graces entry into maturity. Rahner also suggested that the number of sacraments could be changed – by taking Holy Orders out, for example. On the contrary, as happened with Orders and Marriage, Consecration to religious life could be raised to a sacrament; we could also – remembering the Oslo massacre – devise a sacrament to revive trust in God after great catastrophes. . . .

'Fantasies', of course, with no claim to reality. But they are not just caprices, because such reflections point to an essential feature: among all the various signs, the sacraments are those in which the Church, taking account of basic needs, *officially decided* to be present as Church, indicating its existence, reaffirming its faith, and committing its mission.[13] Think of someone who, weighed down with guilt, feels incapable of accepting forgiveness or deciding on a change of life: there may be many aids offered and even needed, from friendly words to communal prayer. But the Church *also* offers a sacrament: it puts together a celebration that makes the God-who-forgives (more) perceptible, stating with absolute certainty that, despite our doubts and indecisions, God does not fail, the community supports, and it is possible to change one's ways.

This shows the importance of *symbols*, since they 'speak' to the depth of our consciousness, bestowing meaning and mobilizing freedom. They are not capricious or arbitrary: baptismal water has no meaning in Orders. But neither are they 'objects' necessarily made up of matter-form – a concept that caused artificial problems for Marriage and Penance. Their significance resides in the whole celebration. One can see that, as they are actions-of-the-Church, it is the Church's task to decide not only the number but also the fundamental *symbolizing* of the sacraments, without leaving them to arbitrary decisions by individual faithful or communities. But it would be a mistake to translate this function into levelling uniformity or dry and sterilizing ritualism. History shows that the basic structure can be adapted to very different ritual forms, historical styles, or cultural sensitivities, since even the most profound and universal symbols have their history, birth, and death.[14] An illuminating question (posed expressly by the Lima Document, no. 28) is: In a culture that has no wheat bread, can rice be less faithful to the eucharistic symbolism than our wafers, which most often evoke white paper rather than real food?

The *opus operatum* affirms the objective certainty of saving Presence. This certainty can only 'take effect' in subjective acceptance, far from all magic and free from confessional disputes. The Church does not ignore human frailty, always prone to failure, routine, and distortion. This is why it protects symbolism, to give greater 'visibility' and 'palpability' to the certainty of the promise,[15] founded on the God-of-Jesus who, creating out of love, has decided to be always with us, nourishing us, supporting us, and saving us. *Infant baptism*, far from being taken as a model, should be interpreted in light of this as an exceptional derivation – not 'magical' transformation in them but grace in the family and community, as places where, as they grow, they can continually discover and live their filiation.[16]

The presence of a *minister* makes visible the commitment of the Church as such. Far from implying a spirit of sacral lordship or ownership, it is clearly seen as a 'service' that coordinates the celebration and re-presents the ecclesial commitment. It also shows that every sacrament (including Penance or Reconciliation) requires a *communal* celebration, presided over by a *minister* (including Marriage).[17] At the same time, as service to the community, the presidency needs to be flexibly open to 'supply' when circumstances – chronic shortage or particular situations – prevent an ordinary minister from being present.

Conclusion

By way of conclusion, I should like to put forward the following observations, simply as *hypotheses*:

The nucleus of sacraments consists in enabling the *acceptance* of grace: the rest is accompaniment and embodiment. These too are important, since the Church is also realized in the realization of the faithful: an authentic acceptance must bring consequences for the community. There is no point in declaring the reality of Reconciliation if sinners do not want to be reconciled to the community, or if the community does not wish to welcome them back. But their re-admission is the declaration – not the cause – of the forgiveness granted by God. My other observations follow this theme.

In an obvious slip (if I understand him well), Rahner wrote that we can talk of Orders and Marriage 'in a reasonable and comprehensible manner without mentioning a bestowal of grace'.[18] If this were taken literally, we should no longer be talking of sacraments. But there is a serious underlying point: sacraments are grace in order to help exceptional circumstances. Take *Marriage*: living it well implies self-giving, attention, faithfulness. . . . But these duties derive from their human nature: they are valid for believers and non-believers; they are not imposed by the sacrament, which consists precisely in being grace to carry them out.[19] This runs counter to the juridicism that so often leads to seeing it as a burden or a trap from which it is then impossible to escape. It also invites consideration of new possibilities, which – not being a Canon Law expert – I simply mention tentatively as a theological possibility.

Historically, the Church decided to unite the validity of Christian marriage to its sacramental celebration. But it does not seem unthinkable that, for pastoral convenience, it might *decide on* a different configuration. To take a common example today, what happens to believers already civilly married who decide to marry in church? If 'marriage is produced by the consent of the parties' (CIC 1057 §1), it would seem thinkable to admit the validity of the civil marriage and focus the *sacrament* on its being grace to live it faithfully.[20] The 'canonical effects' would then be seen as ecclesial confirmation of the implications in the faith community. In present circumstances, we could then also think of a re-configuration that – with some analogy to some 'espousals' – would allow temporary separation between the event of the civil marriage (as a non-sacramental commitment though practised in faith) and the sacramental celebration. An example would be when the contracting partners feel mature enough to live out their marriage with its full consequences for the believing community; this would also be occasion for recognizing its full canonical effects. The freedom with which not only Paul but the evangelists themselves proceeded, introducing exceptions without being bound to Jesus' actual *words*, points to the configuring capacity of the Church being perhaps greater than is generally thought.

All this is tentative and hypothetical. The history of Marriage, however, and the frequent separation between civil and sacramental celebration, is an aid to reflection and can help in the more difficult case of *Holy Orders*. Even so I dare to think that bringing the two together can allow for a distinction between *constitution in ministerial service*, from which the office with its duties and commitments derives, and *sacramental celebration*, as making visible the grace to fulfil these. Even though the two have been brought together historically, it does not seem unthinkable that the Church might have opted for a temporal separation: election–acceptance–office and *later* sacrament. Only historical analysis and theological reflection can judge the reasonableness of this hypothesis. I believe it would be at least worth trying, as it might well, for example, encourage ecumenical dialogue over Anglican Orders, as well as providing greater community participation in the process of election to and confirmation of the office.

There is no space here for general considerations. My hope is that the approach set out above – even with its undoubtedly debatable aspects – can suggest an open, non-exclusive space where the often truly rich and novel advances of present-day theology can be incorporated. I do believe that it at least leads to a greater *coherence*, thanks to its focus from below and its integration of the sacraments in what is most right and undeniable in a culture that rejects all shades of a quasi-miraculous interventionism incompatible with divine transcendence and with legitimate human autonomy.

Translated by Paul Burns

Notes

1. E. Jüngel & C. Ruiz-Garrido, *El ser sacramental*, Salamanca, 2007, p. 9.
2. I shall take account of my own works: 'Os sacramentos hoxe: significado e vivencia', *Encrucillada* 26/127 (2202), pp. 153–76; 'Los sacramentos hoy. Acontecimiento real sin intervencionismo divino', in É. Gaziaux (ed.), *Philosophie et Théologie*. Festschrift Emilio Brito, Leuven, 2007, pp. 458–508.
3. *Frankfurter Rundschau*, 29 July 2011.
4. P. Berger, *A Rumor of Angels: Modern Society and the Rediscovery of the Supernatural*, New York, 1969, rev. 1990 ed., Pelican Books, 1971, pp. 72–3.
5. Jüngel & Ruiz-Garrido, *op. cit.*, p. 16.
6. WA (*Luthers Werke*, Weimarer Ausgabe, 1883–) 6, 86, Th. 18; cf WA 6, 96–7, 24. For the Reformation I follow principally G. Wenz, 'Sakramente I', in *Theologische Realenzyklopädie* 29 (1998), pp. 663–84.
7. What Luther primarily rejected was a false idea of *merit*: '[I]n this sense, in relation to the thing itself, Luther upholds the causality of the sacraments *ex opere operato* and only rejects this causality in the sense of a meritorious understanding of its operation and a saving efficacy without faith' (U. Kühn, *Sakramente*, ²1990, pp. 71ff, cited by G. Wenz, *op. cit.*, pp. 671–2).
8. This took a long time to be accepted, and there was still hard work to be done at Vatican II, as both Rahner and Schillebeeckx noted: see their liberating works *The Church and the Sacraments* (Quaestiones disputatae, New York, 1964; pp. 44–81 in Sp. trans. 1967); *Christ the Sacrament of the Encounter with God*, pp. 88–9.
9. I deal with this subject in some detail in *Recuperar la creación*, Santander, ³2001, chs. 1–3. German translation: Die Wiederentdeckung der Schöpfung, Darmstadt, 2008.
10. K. Barth, *Der Römerbrief*, ²1922 (*The Epistle to the Romans*, London, 1933; Oxford, 1968; here Sp. trans. 1998, p. 54).
11. L.-M. Chauvet, *Symbol and Sacrament*, Collegeville, MN: Pueblo, 1995.
12. Such as STh 3,65,1.
13. I regard Rahner's clarification of this focus as having made a most significant contribution.
14. Cf. M. Eliade, speaking of *hierophanies*: 'Ultimately, we do not know if *something* – object, action, physiological function, being, or game – exists unless it has at some stage, in some place, throughout the history of humankind, been transfigured into hierophany' (*Traité d'histoire des religions / Patterns in Comparative Religions*; here Sp. trans., *Tratado de historia de las religiones*, ²1981, p. 35). P. Tillich insisted repeatedly on the subject.
15. The *promise* has been stressed in Evangelical theology; Catholic theology – in spite of Scotus' strange theory of 'pact' – has perhaps places more stress on *objective* founding in active divine love.
16. St Thomas stated that it could be said of infants: 'they have intention, not through their own actions . . . but through the actions of those who present them' (STh III,68.9, ad 1). Cf. P. Althaus, 'The Church does not baptize all possible children but only the children of Christian parents or those converted to Christianity. It does nor baptize children taken on their own, but as sons and daughters of Christian parents.' (*Die Christliche Wahrheit*, Gütersloh, ⁷1966; p. 553; §56, pp. 550–63, is worth reading).
17. I think the matter-form complication introduced an illogical variant in Marriage, making the 'recipients' the ministers (see my 'O matrimonio como sacramento', *Encrucillada* 30/146 (2006), pp. 5–27). Even the *Catechism of the Catholic Church* (n. 1623) places –

with discreet prudence and without judging – the ministerial presidency of eastern rites alongside the 'habitual' Latin usage.

18. Rahner, *The Church and the Sacraments,* loc. cit., n. 8.

19. The *Code of Canon Law* (1056) says: 'The essential properties of marriage are unity and indissolubility; in Christian Marriage they achieve a distinctive firmness by reason of the sacrament'.

20. *Against this*, one could set the surprise – scandal, for many people – of the Crown Prince of Spain being able to marry, 'normally', a civilly divorced Catholic, because she had not been married 'sacramentally'.

Sacrament Today: The Affirmation of the 'Other'

JOHNSON SILUVAIPILLAI

In this article, from a post-modern perspective, I should like to explore the meaning of sacramental living through the insights of Felix Wilfred and David Power. These two thinkers have provided a significant base from which to reflect on the meaning of the sacraments beyond the rigid limits of pre-Vatican-II sacramentological conceptions. Inspired by the praxis and teaching of the historical Jesus, both these thinkers understand the actualization of the sacramental gift to humanity through the explicit affirmation of the 'Other' – the poor, the oppressed, the alien, and the different. It is interesting to note in this connection that post-modern thinkers such as Emmanuel Levinas call these neglected realities the 'Other'. According to Felix Wilfred and David Power – reflecting from two different geographical regions – the stream of Christian living flows from the sacraments, which is nothing but the emphatic expression of the historical-kenotic commitment of Jesus Christ to the Other, reaching us as gift and grace. The kenosis of Jesus revealed in and through the celebration of the Christian sacraments propels the entire believing community to engage with the Other in order to experience the grace that flows from the bounty of the Divine. The encounter with the Other invites a break with the commercial logic of *do ut des* that underlies the quasi-magical approach to sacraments. It leads us into the realm of pure giving to the Other after the manner of God acting in Jesus Christ and Jesus giving himself to us in total self-emptying.

I The emergence of alterity

The scriptural creation narrative tells us about a God whose entire self is totally intertwined with the heterogenic realities of this universe. This God expresses a sense of fulfilment regarding the goodness that exists within the diverse expressions in creation. 'God saw everything that he had made, and indeed, it was very good' (Gen. 1.31). Hence the biblical God reveals God's own identity through the alterity or the difference that adorns humanity and the entire universe.

Here interdependence, co-existence, and unconditional giving among the multiple realities sound the sacred rhythm of the Divine, which pervades this universe. What we have here is neither the Aristotelian God – 'the unmoved mover' – nor 'self-thinking thought'. But rather we experience a God who is unconditionally interconnected and totally moving with the inner rhythm of every single reality. All this shows how the God of the Bible is radically oriented toward alterity. This alterity is to be seen not only in the uniqueness of every single reality but also in the difference and complementarity it represents. What is true of the nature and universe is reflected also in humanity and in its manifold expressions. We recognize these expressions in religions, cultures, languages, geographical regions, and so on. The alterity, difference, and inter-subjectivity are to be viewed as richness and as an invitation to the practice of love, peace, justice, and truth.

Since alterity characterizes the life-movement of humanity, any exclusion or rejection disrupts its upward movement. According to Levinas, the segregated alterity appears as the 'Other', who does not threaten but whose 'face' cries out for a just response. For Levinas, the Other is nothing but the stranger who cannot be reduced to our representations but has a dimension of transcendence.

> The face with which the Other turns to me is not reabsorbed in a representation of the face. To hear his destitution which cries out for justice is not to represent an image to oneself, but is to posit oneself to be responsible, both as more and as less than the being that presents itself in the face. Less, for the face summons me to my obligation itself and judges me. The being that presents himself in the face comes from a dimension of height, a dimension of transcendence whereby he can present himself as a stranger without opposing me as obstacle or enemy. . . . The Other who dominates me in his transcendence is thus the stranger, the widow, the orphan, to whom I am obligated.[1]

Here the derided and excluded state of the Other becomes the point of ethical learning and commitment.

The Other provides the grammar to understand the sacraments today. For the sacrament is the conjunction between the self and the other, immanence and transcendence. Leonardo Boff's perception of the meaning of Christian sacrament provides further illumination in this regard. For him, '[s]acrament embodies a total experience. No longer is the world divided between immanence and transcendence. . . . The transcendent breaks through into the immanent, transfigures it, and thus makes it transparent.'[2] Thus, the Other as transcendence articulates a new meaning to our existence and reveals the trace of God.

II The kenosis of Jesus and the Other: a sacramental encounter

The encounter with the Other as transcendence presupposes a kenotic existence or self-emptying, something supremely exemplified in the life of Jesus. Kenotic existence is a creative breaking from the narrow confines of the self and a journey toward the Other. Christian sacrament is precisely a *creative breaking* of the eternal Word, its self-emptying to reach out and identify itself with humanity, the Other. David Power sees in the sacraments the locus of the emergence of the Other. Further, the sacrament in its 'celebration and action testifies to the gift of God at work in the world and inviting into the divine communion of Father, Word, and Spirit'.[3]

Wilfred sees this creative breaking in the *historical-kenotic praxis* of the Divine in the concrete commitment of Jesus' identification with the margins (Other) for the welfare of all. He notes:

> In his life, the offer of salvation begins with identification and expands through innumerable acts of his oneness with the people and ends with the communion-meal with the disciples and his supreme sacrifice on the cross where he broke himself totally into the bread of life for the salvation of the world. Jesus' acts in favour of the well being of the people, especially the poor and the marginalized, became sacramental signs of God's identification with us for our well-being.[4]

At this point Wilfred invites us to think much deeper regarding experiencing Jesus as the source of wellbeing of the Other through the sacramental celebrations. He explains this experience from the Hindu theological concept of '*Advaita*'[5] (non-dualism) Vedanta. He perceives the *Advaitic* experience as the source of liberation for all. According to him, it

> leads one to lose one's self in Brahman. One becomes selfless in experiencing one's true self in the other. This interpretation of Advaita as other-centeredness can provide a spiritual foundation for the transformation of the world in love, truth and justice.[6]

Wilfred further envisions the mystery of the Word, which has been unfolding in the sacraments as purely *Advaitic*, because he thinks that the true expression of the mystery of Jesus comes to the fore through his historical engagement with the Spirit of the Divine and the day-to-day life of the people, especially the poor. He affirms,

> The mystery of Jesus does not end in identity with the Ultimate. There is another pole to his mystery: It is his relationship to the mystery of humanity . . . the reinterpretation of Advaita in the light of Christ would imply that the self-atman is not simply one's self, but that the other, one's neighbour is one's very self.[7]

What we can infer from this is that by emptying himself for the Other, Jesus becomes the otherness of the Other, and thus discloses the nearness of God to humanity, which is foundationally a sacramental action. And this act proves the credibility of the kenotic self of Jesus as the source of life and deliverance of the poor. Here the bottom line is, 'Jesus Christ is credible not because of his presumed meta-physical basis, but through Jesus' unconditional love and grace and through his becoming one in solidarity with the poor and embodying in himself the pact of God in defence of the poor'.[8]

Thus Wilfred focuses on the emancipation of the poor (Other) as the locus in which the kenosis of God's Word is unfolded. And this unfolding mystery of Jesus becomes the foundational memory of the believing community. This gives a meaningful understanding of the Christian sacraments and sacramental celebrations. An appealing lead we derive from this is that the poor become a universal-signifying sign through whom God discloses God's identity afresh in every visible oppression of the Other.

According to post-modern thinking, every single unit of this universe is organically connected. The blossoming or withering of one affects the other. Bernard J. Lee believes in such organic-relationship. He says: 'I would stress my profound conviction that we have no merely private destinies as persons or nations, but the destiny of the world is of a piece – not because we have a necessary Meta-story, but because we are interconnected. We live in a system in which whatever happens to any part of the system reverberates in small or large ways throughout the whole system.'[9] Hence, if we relate Lee's concept of interconnected-ness to Wilfred's concept of the poor as the repressed Other in the realm of sacramental celebration, the poor become an interconnecting factor that vibrates the self-giving of the divine through sacramental celebration.

Power, for his part, views the 'local' as the key in experiencing the kenosis of Jesus in and through the celebration of the Christian sacraments. He considers every repressed identity of the local as the 'Other'. Further, for Power, any meaningful and creative breaking of the Word (sacramental celebration) takes place in and through diverse expressions of humanity. He states: 'The language event of Christian sacrament is the event of the Word of God, through the testimony of the Spirit, taking root again, in rich diversity, in time and place.'[10]

This approach by Power takes us to another level of reflection, one that indicates the notion of 'privileging the local'. This notion is vital for any meaningful sacramental celebration. Such a privileging approach questions the totalitarian viewpoint that undermines the uniqueness of plural-local. Moreover, the focus on the local has become a real challenge to the homogenizing-monolithic thought and praxis which intimidate the vulnerable Other in every sphere of contemporary life. In other words, 'the challenge of thinking multiplicity is therefore, in part, one of thinking bodies against abstraction, against universals and generalizations'.[11]

Power further adds that the identity (name) of God is revealed through God's own solidarity with the vulnerable local. According to him, the story of God is a narrative against all abstractions, and it unfolds in and through the mystery of Jesus in the sacramental celebration revealing the name of a self-emptying God. And such giving-self of God exposes the struggle of the local against the homogeneous powers that muzzle its stories. In this connection, Power tells us,

> We can see the Gospel story as a willing abasement, joining it with the image of *kenosis* as it has been examined. The assumption of the form of a slave is the condition of the mission of the Son of man and it is allied with his self-emptying. . . . This emptying of the divine and the divine name before the world, in order to testify to the true name of God, is done in witness before the powers of the world.[12]

For Power, the profound identification of God with humanity in the historical commitment of Jesus for the emancipation of the local comes to the fore through his death on the cross. And this act of God does not reveal God's powerlessness, but rather unveils God's energizing potential that constantly empowers the least and the local. Therefore, for believers, '*kenosis* embraced in communion with the Son in his obedient flesh is not disempowering. It is in fact freeing and energizing. In the drama of his life and death, it was in effect Jesus' identification with sinners and his contestation with powers.'[13]

III Sacramental gift and the Other: a giving without expecting

Christian faith tells us that through sacramental celebration the participants receive the grace and love of God as the sacramental gift. It is a gift, because in sacramental celebration we come to know about the meaning of our own existence through the Other and the God who is becoming the otherness of the Other. And also we experience the mystery of the Divine (Christ-event) as a God-giving. Power conceives every sacramental celebration as *economy of gift*, because God comes to us as a gift to the Other through the self-abasement of Jesus Christ, which indicates the emancipation of the oppressed. He states that in 'gift or gifting [. . .] the accent is placed on the remembrance of Christ's self-emptying love, which through the sacraments enriches those who celebrate. We can write of Sacrament as economy of gift.'[14]

Another important notion recalled here is that the gift we receive through the sacrament is not commercial but 'is the fundamental mystery of love (agape)',[15] in which only the act of giving is in action. In commercial relationships and gifting, expectations are always inherent and may even predominate; the concern is not for the wellbeing of the Other. On this level people connect with other people of the same status. Here gift simply becomes a means. This is not the case with sacraments, where we have a reversal of market relationship and gifting. The words of Louis-Marie Chauvet add clarity to the meaning of sacramental gift (grace). He observes:

> The grace of the sacraments has no value that can be calculated or capitalized upon. It is not a commodity in the market of values and usefulness. Its name, "grace", indicates that it is not an object to be received. [. . .] The grace of the sacraments must be regarded less as 'something' [. . .] than a process of "receiving oneself" as daughter or son, as sister or brother in Christ through the Spirit.[16]

Thus the gift that we receive as the grace of God in the sacraments projects us to another level of engagement: we are led to view our existence as a self-giving to the Other. Power complements the views of Chauvet. For him, the gifts that we share in a celebration and receive should create communion and build community. The strength that we receive as a gift through the sacraments is to empower the Other rather than to remain in our self-centeredness. It is by addressing the unspoken claims of the Other on us that we enrich our existence. Power notes that people who assemble for sacramental celebration,

> bring gifts, in gratitude for what they are and have, in a sense of communion with others, and especially to bring into the assembly the richness of their lives and the depth of their need. They bring gifts that express themselves, the urges and the needs of life, expecting to encounter the urges the needs of others. [. . .] What they bring will be blessed, shared and increased by God's own giving. In the blessing of gifts, it is the life itself that is given increase. An exchange, an economy, is opened up in which God's initiatives outstrips humanity's and brings about a new order.[17]

Wilfred's thinking on sacramental gift may be brought in here to validate the argument of Chauvet and Power and to take us further in our reflections. According to him, considering the sacramental gift of God as the source of empowerment for our own becoming and for the wellbeing of the Other must lead us to a disposition to include and accept the plural nature of reality as a source of strength than a matter of weakness.

> Plurality or diversity is to be welcomed and fostered for what it is – a gift of God to the human family for its enrichment. Therefore exchange among peoples, cultures as well as cross-cultural perspectives, must develop in resolving common issues. Thus pluralism compliments one another so that the other does not become something dispensable or redundant but a must for one's own self-understanding and growth. Genuine pluralism would call also for decentralization of power, wealth, ideology, etc.[18]

In short, plurality meets us as a gift and grace. It opens us up to the Other. Wilfred goes on to say that 'this opening of one's self to the "Other" and in mutual self-giving is the grammar through which we learn the self-gift of God in Jesus Christ for the wellbeing of the world, especially of the poor'.[19] Therefore, through sacramental celebration one receives one's self-giving as a real gift from God and such receiving becomes a reality in each occurrence of the sacrament.

IV From quasi-magical to the manifestation of the realm

The Catechism of Christian Doctrine (known as the Baltimore Catechism) speaks about Catholic sacramental doctrine in the following manner:

> Q. 136. What is a sacrament?
> A. A sacrament is an outward sign instituted by Christ to give grace.
> Q. 138. Whence have the sacraments the power of giving grace?
> A. The sacraments have the power of giving grace from the merits of Jesus Christ.[20]

The understanding of sacrament behind these questions and answers is abstract and a-historical. It lacks any reference to concrete human realities and experiences. Here the participation of a believing community, its meaningful response, and its mystery are also not articulated. Such an a-historical and non-experiential approach may lead a believer to perceive the meaning of the Christian sacraments in a quasi-magical way. In the present context of plurality, suffering, and oppression, any quasi-magical understanding of sacraments cannot bring about the real meaning of the kenotic praxis of Jesus celebrated in the sacraments.

In order to overcome the danger of any magical understanding of sacraments, we need to underline the reality of community, besides the reality of the Other and of the gift. The community itself is to be viewed as an enlightened community of self-awareness oriented to the reality of the Other. Wilfred, in fact, perceives this sacramental body – the Church – as the body of enlightenment. As an awakened body it manifests the kenosis of Jesus through its commitment to the Other. It mirrors the awakening and enlightenment of Jesus toward the Other:

> Church is viewed as the community of those who are awakened to the divine mystery, to the *logos* shining forth in the hearts of persons. It is the community of those who, as a result of the inner awakening, are integrated with others and in harmony with nature and the whole universe. In correlation to this inner experience, we have in the exterior realm the mystery of the *logos* as experienced in the historical figure Jesus, in his life, teachings, death and resurrection.[21]

This makes clear that, as an enlightened and awakened body, the church community will be a body listening to and dialoguing with and opening up itself to the Other. As it lends its ears to the story of Christ in sacramental celebration, it has to listen to the voice of the Other, the testimonies of other religions and cultures. As Jesus authenticated his sacramental living through his commitment on the cross, the Church also must ratify its sacramentality through its solidarity with the repressed identities. It is through this whole process that the church community will progress from a magical to a real understanding of sacrament.

Conclusion

I have sought here to reflect on sacrament through the perspective of the Other and through the key concept of gift, both of which took us to the kenotic praxis of historical Jesus. Jesus who becomes the otherness of the Other in and through sacramental celebration brings us face to face with the repressed Other. The sacramental celebration takes us to the realm of self-giving and through this to discover the otherness of the Other. The prevalent quasi-magical understanding of sacraments needs to be overcome by referring to historical realities and experiences and by creating an awakened and enlightened community. The faith community, which is the sacramental body of Christ, confirms its credibility not merely through its proclamation of the Glad Tidings of the Word, but through its commitment to transcend its confines in order to reach out to the Other. All this tells us that the manifestation of the real cannot be experienced by remaining in the glow of mere metaphysical expressions, but by committing ourselves to the emancipation of the repressed-Other here and now.

Notes

1. Emmanuel Levinas, *Totality and Infinity*, trans. Alphonso Lingis, Pittsburgh, PA: Duquesne University Press, 1969, p. 215. See also Robert Bernasconi, 'The Alterity of the Stranger and the Experience of the Alien', in *The Face of the Other and the Trace of God: Essays on the Philosophy of Emmanuel Levinas*, ed. Jeffrey Bloechl, New York: Fordham University Press, 2000, pp. 62–3.
2. Leonardo Boff, *Sacraments of Life, Life of the Sacraments*, trans. John Drury, Portland, OR: Pastoral Press, 1987, pp. 24–5.
3. David N. Power, *Sacrament: The Language of God's Giving*, New York: Crossroad, 1999, p. 87.
4. Felix Wilfred, *The Sling of Utopia*, Delhi: ISPCK, 2005, p. 308.
5. 'Advaita: (*a-dvaita*, 'non dualism') the doctrine of monism, which teaches that only the Ultimate Principle is integral, whole and "unsplit" (*abheda*). This Ultimate Principle alone has real existence and all phenomena are either illusive (*maya*) or ephemeral, although the illusion may be dispelled by insight or knowledge (*jnana*). The term is used in opposition to *dvaita* (or *Bheda*), a dualism which holds that the Soul, of which the individual soul is a part, is a separate principle, with an independent existence of its own, and is only associated with or stands in particular relation to the Ultimate Principle. In other words, that there are two internal realities, the Ultimate Principle and the Soul. [. . .] The Vedanta, especially of *Sankara*, [. . .] was a strictly non-dualistic concept, recognizing only *Brahman* and categorically negating the existence of the individual soul.' Benjamin Walker, *Hindu World: An Encyclopedia Survey of Hinduism*, New Delhi: Munshiram Manoharlal, pp. 5–6.
6. Felix Wilfred, *Beyond Settled Foundations*, Madras: Department of Christian Studies, University of Madras, 1993, p. 219.
7. Felix Wilfred, *Beyond Settled Foundations*, p. 193.
8. Wilfred, 'Christianity between Decline and Resurgence', *Concilium* 2005/3, p. 31.
9. Bernard J. Lee, 'The Only Survivable World: A Post-modern Systems Approach to a Religious Intuition', in *Sacred Interconnections: Post-modern Spirituality, Political Economy,*

and Art, ed. David Ray Griffin, Albany, NY: State University Press of New York, 1990, p. 51.
10. Power, *Sacrament: The Language of God's Giving*, p. 87.
11. Laurel C. Schneider, *Beyond Monotheism: A Theology of Multiplicity*, New York: Routledge, Taylor and Francis, 2008, p. 142.
12. David N. Power, *Love without Calculation: A Reflection on Divine Kenosis*, New York: Crossroad, 2005, p. 27.
13. Power, 'On What Foundations? The Christian Witness to the Justice of the Divine Trinity', *Theoforum* 34 (2003), p. 172.
14. Power, *Sacrament: The Language of God's Giving*, p. 11.
15. Lambert J. Leijssen, *With the Silent Glimmer of God's Spirit: A Post-modern Look at the Sacraments*, trans. Marie Baird, Mahwah, NJ: Paulist Press, 2006, p. 33.
16. Louis-Marie Chauvet, *The Sacraments: The Word of God at the Mercy of the Body*, trans. Madeleine Beaumont, Collegeville, MN: Liturgical Press, 1997, pp. 88–9.
17. David N. Power, *Sacrament: The Language of God's Giving*, pp. 316–7.
18. Felix Wilfred, *Sunset in the East? Asian Challenges and Christian Involvement*, Madras: University of Madras, 1991, p. 142.
19. Wilfred, *The Sling of Utopia*, p. 309.
20. 'A Catechism of Christian Doctrine', in George S. Worgul (ed.), *From Magic to Metaphor: A Validation of Christian Sacraments*, Mahwah, NJ: Paulist Press, 1980, p. 14.
21. Wilfred, *Beyond Settled Foundations*, pp.197–8.

The Liturgical Profundity of the Ethically Mundane

BEN KAUTZER

At the heart of prophetic witness in scripture is a deep concern for the poor and the oppressed – the lowly dwellers huddled at the margins of our collective perception. This concern carries with it a sharp and unsettling critique of those who would audibly declare God's praises and yet deny with their hands the plight of the needy.

In the face of human suffering, injustice, loneliness, and alienation, the Church today is confronted with the permanent ambiguities of its vocation to be in and for the world a worshipping community disciplined in the costly habits of cruciform love. Underlying this vocation is a restless and uncomfortable tension between liturgy and ethics, sacrifice and mercy. Theological debates surrounding this question continue to receive scholarly attention, but not always with fully satisfying results. Despite a growing consensus that the 'liturgy of the church' and the 'liturgy of the neighbour' are somehow bound up with one another, discerning the nature of their mutual inseparability remains an open and contested question. Within many academic approaches, an unfortunate methodological fixation on a word/sacrament binary has far too often (and far too willingly) relegated the Church's ministry of charity to the supplemental margins of 'practical theology'. Left unqualified, such subtle demarcations risk supplanting discipleship with a kind of volunteerism as the normative framework orienting Christian ministry in the contemporary world.

In *Deus Caritas Est*, Pope Benedict XVI challenges such dichotomizations with a more nuanced and integrated vision of the Church's life. He writes,

> The Church's deepest nature is expressed in her *three-fold* respons-

> ibility: of proclaiming the word of God (*kerygma-martyria*), celebrating the sacraments (*leitourgia*), and exercising the ministry of charity (*diakonia*). These duties presuppose each other and are inseparable. For the Church, charity is not a kind of welfare activity which could equally well be left to others, but is a part of her nature, an indispensible expression of her very being.[1]

Affording the ministry of charity equal ecclesiological weight as both word *and* sacrament, Benedict XVI seems to suggest that the works of mercy and justice constitute not merely what the Church *does,* but what the Church *is*; not its relevant *usefulness,* but its vulnerable *faithfulness*.

Drawing on work of Edward Schillebeeckx and Louis-Marie Chauvet, in what follows, I shall attempt a theological re-imagining of this triadic deep-structure (word–sacrament–charity) from the perspective of sacramentality. In particular, I shall argue that the 'works of mercy' (i.e. gifts of food and drink, prayer and compassion, shelter and hospitality) name concrete sites in which the Church's sacramentality, ethics, and prophetic witness converge. In other words, these mundane, seemingly insignificant acts constitute what we might call a *liturgically-shaped politics of the everyday*.

I Edward Schillebeeckx: reconceiving liturgy and ethics sacramentally

In his groundbreaking work *Christ the Sacrament of the Encounter with God* (1960), Edward Schillebeeckx helped inaugurate a paradigm shift in sacramental theology.[2] Resisting the scholastic temptation simply to secure the number, institution, and efficacy of the seven sacraments administered by the hierarchical Church, Schillebeeckx pursued an alternative point of departure in the very notion of 'sacramentality' itself. In this view, the entire Christian life participates in the deeper, primordial sacraments of Christ and Church. Jesus in his humanity – as 'supreme worship of the Father' and the incarnational manifestation of grace – is *the* sacrament of God.[3] As the ecclesial prolongation of the incarnation, the Church in its visibility is the basic sacrament of Christ and Kingdom. The Church celebrates explicitly the grace of God otherwise implicit and hidden in all human life. One of Schillebeeckx's most important contributions is his insistence on the *evental* character of sacraments. Sacraments are not so much objects or things, but rather acts – personal and salvific *encounters* with Christ as mystery. However, the intelligibility of any particular sacramental encounter depends entirely upon this fundamental sacramental milieu.

This new perspective provoked Schillebeeckx to consider the (re)discovery of other sacramental sites of encounter beyond the walls of the Church. He began to explore the idea of liturgical ethic of love and justice in the midst of everyday life. Though the administration of the seven sacraments manifests Christ's sacramental presence *par excellence*, Schillebeeckx nonetheless concludes that: 'For all men, encounters with their fellow men are the sacrament of encounter with God.'[4] Indeed, by suggesting that ethical practice is itself *worship*, in *Christ the Sacrament*, the tension between liturgy and ethics is worked out in terms of 'the sacramental and the extra-sacramental bestowal of grace'.[5] Sacraments of the Church become 'necessary as markers, milestones on the way, so that by living the Christian life *as a whole* we may become more and more one with Christ'.[6]

Despite the suggestive tone of these theological explorations, Schillebeeckx's early project ultimately remains within a conventional sacramental orientation. His 'extra-sacramental bestowals of grace' are radically subordinated to the seven ecclesially administered rites. This comes to the surface in a revealing summative analogy given toward the end of *Christ the Sacrament*. Schillebeeckx likens the sacramentality of the Church to concentric circles emanating from a stone tossed into a pond: 'The ripples flow in all directions from this one central point. This point is the Church, the visible presence of Christ's grace on earth, and from it all movement can be seen to flow.' These ripples represent an explicit hierarchy of value beginning with the Eucharist and then expanding outward in descending order to the other six sacraments, the word, all human conduct which proceeds from grace, and into the entire world of humanity. While word, sacraments, and charity may be 'visible realities in this world of which the Lord avails himself, using his rich fund of inspiration in the most diverse means, to orientate man existentially towards God in Jesus Christ', they nonetheless become less potent and clearly defined the farther their circles emanate out from the Church.[7] So while Schillebeeckx's early work laid some key foundations for conceiving all the world as shot-through with the grace of God, in the end his understanding of sacramentality was simply insufficiently sacramental when it came to the status of ethical praxis as sacrifice, worship, and praise.

Not long after publishing *Christ the Sacrament,* Schillebeeckx picked up this problem again in a lesser know work, *God the Future of Man* (1968). Confronted with an emerging post-war 'Christian atheism', Schillebeeckx wrestles afresh with question of what authentic liturgy looks like in light of the existential demands of ethical practice. Are these simply two worlds which run alongside one another in parallel disjunction? To the contrary, Schillebeeckx responds that 'from the Christian point of view, the cleave between worldly activity and liturgical worship is a disaster, and this gap must be bridged'.[8] The question is: how?

Abandoning his earlier language of 'extra-sacramental grace', Schillebeeckx proposes a new way forward with what he calls 'secular worship'. By this he intends something like a sacramental structure in the midst of the everyday – an implicit modality of rendering glory to God through caritative acts of ethical dispossession. As with formal liturgical rites, Schillebeeckx insists that 'secular worship' is itself grounded in the primordial sacramentality of Jesus. However, this idea is now developed in a different direction. 'Calvary was not a church liturgy', writes Schillebeeckx, 'but an hour of human life, which Jesus experienced as worship. In it, our redemption is to be found. We have not been redeemed by an act of pure worship, a liturgical service – our redemption was accomplished by an act which was part of Jesus' human life, situated in history and in the world.'[9] It is precisely through this sacramentalizing of history in the incarnational materiality of Jesus *in the world* that a 'new concept of worship came into being – human life itself experienced as liturgy or worship of God'.[10] Schillebeeckx is clear that this 'spiritual worship' (Rom. 12.1–2) takes concrete form, not as object, but as particular acts of compassion, hospitality, and solidarity. Works of mercy and justice are at once true sacrifices holy and pleasing to God (Isa. 58; Phil. 2.17, 4.18; Heb. 13.16) and sites of sacramental encounter with the hidden presence of Christ in the least (Prov. 19.17; Matt. 25.31–46). In his later writings, Schillebeeckx suggests that such compassionate encounters arising from situations of destitution, exploitation, abandonment, and despair confront us more as sacramental 'disturbances' than consolations, provoking us to responsive engagement.[11]

Schillebeeckx is very clear that 'secular worship and Christian liturgy are not alternatives – they are two complementary, mutually evocative forms of the one Christianity'.[12] This mutuality determines the fundamental orientation of both. 'Without secular worship, prayer and the Church's liturgy, our speaking of and to God become simply an ideological superstructure without roots in the realities of life, and hence artificial.' He goes on to write: 'Without secular worship, the Christian Eucharist itself becomes meaningless for us.' For church liturgy 'realizes itself in love and concern for our fellow-men'.[13] To borrow from Nicholas Wolterstorff, we could say that here Schillebeeckx's theology shifts from a rather vague *both/and* juxtaposition of liturgy and ethics in *Christ the Sacrament* to a far more radical *not/unless* framework – *not* authentic liturgy *unless* mercy and justice.[14] Instead of imagining emanating concentric circles, perhaps it would be better to think this inseparability in terms of a single sacramental *ordo* – 'a definite, qualified manner of being in the world' – constituted by a complex and oscillating movement between eucharistic gathering and missional sending.

Schillebeeckx's explorative theology makes possible a sacramental reimagining of Benedict XVI's ecclesiological triad. Word, sacrament, and charity hold together as personal sites of sacramental encounter located within the wider fabric of the Church's liturgical existence. However, many of Schillebeeckx's initial positions require further development. For a more robust elucidation of the inner coherence of word–sacrament–charity we must now turn to the work of Chauvet.

II Louis-Marie Chauvet: the liturgy of the neighbour

Louis-Marie Chauvet is rapidly emerging as one of the most significant sacramental theologians of the twenty-first century. In Kevin Irwin's estimation, 'Chauvet will exercise in the next decades the same kind of wide-ranging and theologically profound influence which the early Schillebeeckx wielded about the sacraments from the early 1960s on'.[15]

In his *magnum opus*, *Symbol and Sacrament: A Sacramental Reinterpretation of Christian Existence*, Chauvet proposes an ambitious theological agenda: to rethink the whole of Christian identity from the perspective of what he calls a 'fundamental sacramentality' of symbolic mediation.[16] Chauvet shifts the focus away from how sacraments 'work', and instead begins from the presupposition that the entire life of faith is '*always-already inscribed in the order of the sacramental*'.[17] From this point of departure, he sees the Church as itself a sacramentally constituted symbolic order with its own nexus of language, knowledge, meaning, ritual, and praxis. It is within this polyvalent *milieu* that the believing subject is born and through which this subjectivity is given a body in the world.[18]

Among Chauvet's most valuable insights is his discovery that the deep-structure of Christian subjectivity unfolds as a series of connections between three distinct, yet mutually defining elements: scripture (the level of cognition), sacrament (the level of thanksgiving), and ethics (the level of action).[19] This tripod represents levels of mediation through which the Church's faith is negotiated. Together these three give the sacramental system its structural coherence. In one sense, scripture–sacrament–ethics each describe broad horizons containing multiple dimensions. Yet at a basic anthropological level, they point toward what it means to *conceive*, *celebrate*, and *live* within a particular 'world' of symbolic meaning.

As part of the symbolic order of the Church, 'scripture' names the proclamation of the 'founding event' of God's saving *gift* of mercy in Jesus Christ. This declaration of good news involves not only the Bible, but also preaching, theology, catechesis, and tradition – all of which bear witness to this past gift 'where God extends God's grace [. . .] in the *historical and henceforth glorious body of Christ*'.[20]

'Sacrament' refers to the various liturgical forms of celebration through which the Church participates in and *receives* this gift of God's promise in its own present life. Through sacramental rites, particularly Baptism and Eucharist, the Church enters into and performs the narrative drama of Jesus' risen life. Such rituals are '*the symbolic place of the on-going transition between scripture and ethics, from the letter to the body*'.[21] As doxology in ritual form, sacraments include 'everything that pertains to the thankfulness which the Church expresses to God'.[22]

All too often in sacramental theology word and sacrament congeal into a closed circuit: *lex orandi, lex credendi.* However, for Chauvet 'ethics' (*lex agendi*) belongs to the very defining logic of sacramentality. The living conduct by which 'Christians testify to the gospel by their actions' is best understood as embodied gratitude.[23] Chauvet explains:

> the *sacramental rendering-thanks* seeks to be enfleshed in the *living-in-grace* among brothers and sisters. This ethical dimension is not simply an extrinsic consequence of the eucharistic process; it belongs to it as an *intrinsic* element. […] [I]t is precisely ethics that must become authentically "eucharistic." Grace is always bestowed as a task; and the sacramental body, as an injunction to give to the Risen One this body made of the world that he requires of us.[24]

With this in mind, it is clear that these elements are not simply static 'things', but rather identify an architectonic dynamism of symbolic gift-exchange. Drawing upon the anthropological theories of Marcel Mauss, Chauvet demonstrates that the inter-relationship among scripture–sacrament–ethics is also a continual process of gift–reception–return. Mauss famously demonstrated that ritual 'symbolic exchange' functions differently from the utilitarian logic of market exchange; a true gift can only be received as a gift through a thankful response, a further giving in return.[25] Thus the gift of God's redemptive life is ritually received in the sacraments. However, this 'reception' is only a true reception to the extent that the Church responds with a return-gift of praise and thanksgiving manifested in justice, liberation, mercy, forgiveness. Ethics is not simply a moral appendance tacked on to worship – as if worship were simply an *instrument* for the *production* of 'good behaviour'. On the contrary, Chauvet's work presupposes a *not/unless* perspective resonant with Schillebeeckx:

> [W]ithout the return-gift of an *ethical* practice by which the subject 'verifies' what it has received in the sacrament, Christian identity would be stillborn. […] Consequently, just as the liturgy itself must become the object of an ethical reinterpretation to become fully Christian, so also, and conversely, an ethics which is not reinterpreted liturgically, that is to say, as a theological response to the initial grace from God – as generous as it might be – would lose its Christian identity (1. Cor. 13.1–3).[26]

This analysis enables us to understand that when Chauvet speaks of this ethical element as a 'liturgy of the neighbour', he is referring to far more than a shallow juxtaposition. Christian ethics is simply not thinkable in isolation from word and sacrament. Likewise – and this is important to remember – word and sacrament are equally unintelligible when bifurcated from the ministry of charity. It is true that a permanent temptation is simply to fixate on any one of these elements. Indeed, too many of the theological dead-ends we regularly encounter stem from tipping this balance in one direction to the exclusion of another (resulting in either fundamentalism, sacramental magic, or moralism).[27] Scripture–sacrament–ethics do indeed 'presuppose each other and are inseparable' precisely to the extent that they constitute the sacramentality of Christian identity itself.[28]

III Liturgical extensity and sacramental intensity

For all the strengths of Chauvet's sacramental theology (and there are many), I do wonder to what extent he has unwittingly covered over a fundamental problem concerning this 'liturgy of the neighbour'. As we have seen, Chauvet reads scripture–sacrament–ethics in fairly sweeping terms. These are general categories or orientations. It might be more precise to describe them, employing a conceptual framework from Daniel Hardy, as a kind of liturgical 'extensity', or diffused 'spread-out-ness'. In this way, we can think of sacramentality as a horizon within which particular sites of sacramental 'intensity' can emerge.[29] For example, what we have been calling the 'liturgy of the Church' is a kind of extensity encompassing all sorts of things: prayers, words, gestures, sounds, colours, smells, tastes, sacraments, processions, buildings, actions, people, and so forth.[30] 'Sacramentality' is itself extensity. However, within this liturgical 'spread-out-ness', the sacraments themselves, especially the Eucharist, name those particular counterpoint moments of 'intensity' or 'personal encounter' and 'communion' with the risen Christ.

Now this use of extensity in sacramental theology since the early 1960s has proven incredibly effective in challenging scholastic reductionism, attending more fully to the phenomenological milieu of actual embedded liturgical situations, and, of course, exploring some of the wider structural relationships I have been discussing throughout this essay.

That being said, sacramental extensity (or sacramentality as such) left on its own inevitably tends toward theological abstraction, arbitrariness, and ultimately varying degrees of incoherence. Nowhere is this more evident than in discussions of the liturgy of the neighbour. Whether it is called secular worship, or liturgy of the world, or liturgy of the other, or simply liturgy of life, the phrase by definition denotes a liturgical and ethical extensity. However, unlike the liturgy of the Church, the liturgy of the neighbour is rarely afforded corresponding sites of intensity.

In *Christ the Sacrament*, Schillebeeckx succumbs to this abstraction when he writes of 'the Christian life itself as sacrament of the encounter with God', and that even the ethical encounter of '*all* men' with their fellow men is 'the sacrament of encounter with God'.[31] His analogy of the pond further demonstrates how sacramental 'intensity' remains fundamentally within the liturgy of *Church*, not the neighbour. In a similar way, Chauvet's general claim that 'ethics' refers to literally 'all that pertains to *action* in the name of the gospel' is uncomfortably vague. To be fair to Chauvet, it must be said that the final agenda of his book is to write a theology of the sacraments (in their intensity), having first established the wider extensive sacramentality of the faith itself. Nonetheless, considering the importance Chauvet places on the inherent dependence of word and sacrament on ethics, it is problematic how ambiguous his liturgy of the neighbour actually is.

We can see the potential problems with unfettered extensity much more clearly in the hyperbolic sacramental theology of Leonardo Boff. In his provocative book *Sacraments of Life, Life of the Sacraments*, Boff firmly challenges reductionism, writing that 'the seven sacraments do not swallow up all the sacramental richness of the Church. Everything the Church does has a sacramental density because the Church is fundamentally a sacrament. [. . .] Anything can be a sacramental vehicle of divine grace'.[32] Quite literally, everything and anything can be sacramental: Boff's family mug, his father's cigarette butt, homemade bread, a Christmas candle, an autobiography, a schoolteacher, a promised word. Ironically, Boff does have intensive notions available (i.e. 'density'), yet he deploys this language in a purely extensive manner.

While we have much to learn from Boff's text, it does demonstrate what can happen when sacramentality becomes unhinged from its moorings. As William Cavanaugh puts it, 'this attempt to re-enchant the secular world, however, only leaves the world more bereft of God. If God always stands "behind" signs, then signs become interchangeable, and God never truly saturates any particular sign'.[33] I take this recurring ambiguity as a signal that sacramental theologians on the whole have not yet fully come to terms with what ethical sacramentality demands of our thinking.

IV The liturgical profundity of the works of mercy

If we are to take seriously the tension between liturgy and ethics and if we are to use the language of sacramentality to do so, my final question is this: what are these 'saturated signs'? Where are these moments of sacramental intensity to be found within the liturgy of the neighbour? In what kind of ethical act might we discover 'strong moments' of God's self-disclosure?[34]

Theologians seeking such 'strong moments' in the mundane patterns of daily life can find no better place to begin than Matthew 25.31–46. The passage depicts the Son of Man taking the throne of heaven as King and Judge before the gathered nations. The King addresses the righteous saying, 'I was hungry and you gave me something to eat, I was thirsty and you gave me something to drink, I was a stranger and you invited me in' (25.35–6). Taken aback in bewilderment they reply, 'Lord, when did we see you hungry or thirsty or welcome you?' The King answers them, 'What you did unto the least of these brothers of mine, you did unto me' (25.40).

In his meditations on the mediated 'presences' of Christ, Jürgen Moltmann discerns in this passage a parallel Christological identification: first, with the apostolic mission of the believers – 'whoever hears you hears me' (John 12.44); and second, with the least of Christ's brethren – 'whoever visits them visits me' (Matt. 25.36). Moltmann asks whether the Church can 'exist in the truth and presence of Christ if it does not link this mission and this expectation together and, acting in the presence of the exalted one, seek the fellowship of the crucified one in the poor'?[35] This is an important question. Earlier I spoke of liturgy and ethics as single sacramental *ordo* oscillating between eucharistic gathering and missional sending. Moltmann is clear that in the Eucharist the exalted Christ is present to his Church in sacramental intensity. What is more, he argues that amidst this missional sending into the world the crucified Christ confronts us in the bodily mediation of the neighbour. This double brotherhood of Christ thus names a double sacramentality.

If the Church were to take seriously the implications of the exalted *and* crucified presence, '[t]hen the Church with its mission would be present where Christ awaits it, amid the downtrodden, the sick and the captives. The apostolate says what the Church is. The least of Christ's brethren say where the Church belongs.'[36]

As Schillebeeckx has taught us, sacramentality is first and foremost act, event, and encounter. Matthew 25 narrates an *act* of mercy and compassion, an *event* of solidarity between persons in a situation of need, and an *encounter* with the veiled presence of Christ crucified. For Chauvet, the Christological identification with the practice of mercy and justice suggests 'a kind of "sacrament" of the Risen One'.[37] Despite his hesitancy, Chauvet does go on to say that 'the prime location of liturgy or sacrifice for Christians is the ethics of everyday life by theological faith and charity'.[38]

It seems to me that Chauvet and Schillebeeckx are both, in various ways, reaching, feeling toward a reality of immense theological significance. It is Hans Urs von Balthasar who hits the nail squarely on the head. He writes that in his unique and concrete particularity the neighbour standing before me

> becomes the bearer of God's call, the Sacrament of the word of God as it comes to me. This Sacrament is dispensed in daily life, not in the church; in conversation, not during a sermon. It is administered not in prayer and meditation, but in situations where prayer shows that it is genuine and where meditation results in the apostolate. There it will be decided whether I have really heard God's word in my prayer, whether I have received his Body and Blood in church effectively. And the decision is made in the right way, if it is evident that I am willing to give my neighbor the bread and wine of the word and of my own life.[39]

Conclusion

When we pull together the various threads that weave the sacramental context in which the works of mercy fit, then it becomes clear that these practices belong at the heart of this liturgy of the neighbour. However, they do so in a rather particular way. And this is the whole point, really. I would argue that what the Eucharist is to the liturgy of the Church, the works of mercy are to the liturgy of the neighbour – that is, sites of sacramental intensity in which we are drawn into a redemptive encounter with the veiled presence of Christ. In typical provocative simplicity, Mother Teresa writes, 'In the Eucharist, I see Christ in the appearance of bread. In the slums, I see Christ in the distressing guise of the poor – in the broken bodies, in the children, in the dying. That is why this work becomes possible.'[40]

What these humble practices of compassion invoke is an invitation to *abide*. In John's Gospel Jesus tells his disciples, 'I am the vine; you are the branches. […] No branch can bear fruit by itself; it must remain in the vine. […] If you obey my commands, you will remain in my love […]. My command is this: Love each other as I have loved you' (John 15.1–12). As the scriptures bear witness, Christ, the true vine, is the gratuitous source from which life flows; yet for life to be received, one must *remain* in the life-giver. For John the primary locus of this remaining is neither a mere confession of faith nor an internal existential experience, but in the extending outward of grace, that is, in the re-giving of the gifts of charity. Paradoxically, the gift of grace is received only through the modality of openness and giving again. This liturgical *ordo* of mercy is nothing less than a *habitus* of inhabitation – a remaining in the gift through our own kenotic dispossession – a return of thanksgiving given flesh through the bodily mediation of the neighbour.

Notes

1. Benedict XVI, *God is Love*, San Francisco: Ignatius Press, 2006, p. 60. Emphasis added.
2. Edward Schillebeeckx, *Christus, Sacrament van de Godsontmoeting*, Bilthoven: H. Nelissen, 1960. Eng. *Christ the Sacrament of the Encounter with God*, trans. C. Ernst, New York: Sheed & Ward, 1963. For a detailed overview of these developments in Roman Catholic sacramental theology, see Kenan B. Osborne, *Sacraments in a Postmodern World: A Theology of the Third Millennium*, Mahwah, NJ: Paulist Press, 1999, pp. 5–40.
3. *Ibid.*, pp. 15, 29.
4. *Ibid.*, p. 206.
5. *Ibid.*, pp. 197–8.
6. *Ibid.*, p. 200. Emphasis original.
7. *Ibid.*, pp. 215–6. For a critical assessment, see Aloysius Pieris, *An Asian Theology of Liberation*, Maryknoll, NY: Orbis Books, 1988, p. 12.
8. Schillebeeckx, 'Secular Worship and Church Liturgy', in *God the Future of Man*, trans. N. D. Smith, London: Sheed & Ward, 1968: pp. 91–116: here 96.

9. *Ibid.*, p. 99.
10. *Ibid.*, p. 100.
11. See Susan A. Ross, 'Church and Sacraments', in *The Praxis of the Reign of God: An Introduction to the Theology of Edward Schillebeeckx*, ed. Mary Catherine Hilkert & Robert J. Schreiter, New York: Fordham University Press, 2002, pp. 133–48.
12. Schillebeeckx, 'Secular Worship', p. 108.
13. *Ibid.*, pp. 107, 108. 'Secular activity is a part of the eucharistic sacrifice. Indeed, as for Jesus himself, so for the Christian, the "spiritual sacrifice" of everyday life in the world with one's fellow-men is *the* sacrifice that matters; it is in this life in the world that the Christian finds the *reality* of his living participation in the sacrifice of Christ, the sacramental form of which he may receive as nourishment in the Eucharist, as his confession in faith that secular worship is only possible by virtue of God's "new creation" in Christ' (p. 114).
14. See Nicholas Wolterstorff, 'Justice as a Condition of Authentic Liturgy', *Theology Today* 48 (1991), pp. 6–21. In an earlier work, *Until Justice and Peace Embrace*, Grand Rapids: Eerdmans, 1983, Wolterstorff contends that it is not ethics in general, but the works of mercy that define the core of this *not/unless* structure: 'If worship is performed, but the works of mercy and justice are missing, then a shadow is cast over the worship, and its authenticity is brought into question. For this very same God whom we are to worship by celebrating his deeds in memorial also requires of us that, in grateful response to those deeds, we take heed of him by doing the works of mercy and justice. But can we not also say that if the works of mercy and justice are performed but the worship is missing, then a shadow is cast over those works, and *their* authenticity is brought into question? For this very same God, whom we are to heed by doing works of mercy and justice in gratitude for those deeds of his that we remember and expect, also requires of us that we celebrate in memorial of those deeds: work and worship are mutually authenticating' (pp. 156–7).
15. Kevin W. Irwin, 'The *petit* Chauvet on the Sacraments', *Antiphon* 6.3 (2001), pp. 49–54, here 49.
16. Louis-Marie Chauvet, *Symbol and Sacrament: A Sacramental Reinterpretation of Christian Existence*, trans. Patrick Madigan & Madeleine Beaumont, Collegeville, MN: Liturgical Press, 1987, p. 1.
17. *Ibid.*, p. 155.
18. *Ibid.*, pp. 178–80.
19. *Ibid.*, p. 160. Chauvet's analysis of this triad is unprecedented in its nuance and sophistication. Each element names a wide horizon of meaning, which, taken together, weave the fabric Christian being in the world in its full personal and corporate dimensions. Sketched in a more detailed yet summary fashion, Chauvet's structure also includes:
Scripture = gift/Christ's historical and glorious body/past/knowledge/cognition/sign: conceiving a world;
Sacraments = reception/Christ's eucharistic body/present/gratitude/recognition/symbol: celebrating a world; and
Ethics = return-gift/Christ's ecclesial body/future/action/praxis/practice: living in a world.
20. *Ibid.*, p. 279.
21. *Ibid.*, p. 265.
22. Chauvet, *The Sacraments: The Word of God at the Mercy of the Body*, Collegeville, MN: Liturgical Press, p. 30.
23. *Ibid.*, p. 31.
24. *Ibid.*, pp. 277–8.
25. See Marcel Mauss, *The Gift: Forms and Functions of Exchange in Archaic Societies*, trans. Ian Cunnison, London: Cohen & West, 1966.

26. Chauvet, *Symbol and Sacrament*, p. 281. Emphasis original.
27. *Ibid.*, pp. 273–7.
28. See Cesare Giraudo, 'The Eucharist as *Diakonia*: From the Service of Cult to the Service of Charity', in *Liturgy in a Postmodern World*, ed. Keith F. Pecklers, SJ, London: Continuum, 2003, pp. 102–32.
29. Daniel Hardy, *Finding the Church: The Dynamic Truth of Anglicanism*, London: SCM Press, 2001, pp. 109–13.
30. For a fascinating analysis of how significant this liturgical 'extensity' is for our understanding of sacramental 'intensity,' see L.-M.Chauvet, 'The Liturgy in its Symbolic Space', in *Liturgy and the Body,* ed. L.-M. Chauvet & F. K. Lumbala, *Concilium* 1995/3, pp. 29–39.
31. Schillebeeckx, *Christ the Sacrament*, pp. 200, 206.
32. Leonardo Boff, *Sacraments of Life, Life of the Sacraments*, trans. John Drury, Washington: The Pastoral Press, 1987, p. 5. One does wonder to what extent Boff's text would have benefitted from a more careful distinction between sacrament in particular and metaphor or symbol more generally.
33. William T. Cavanaugh, *Torture and Eucharist: Theology, Politics, and the Body of Christ*, Oxford: Blackwell, 2000, pp. 13–14.
34. Kevin W. Irwin, 'A Sacramental World – Sacramentality as the Primary Language for Sacraments', *Worship* 76.3 (May 2002), pp. 197–211, here 198.
35. Jürgen Moltmann, *The Church in the Power of the Holy Spirit: A Contribution to Messianic Ecclesiology*, London: SCM Press, 1977, p. 127.
36. *Ibid.*, p. 129.
37. Chauvet, *Symbol and Sacrament*, p. 166.
38. *Ibid.*, p. 262.
39. Hans Urs von Balthasar, 'The Sacrament of the Brother', in *The Question of God and Modern Man*, New York: Seabury, 1967, pp. 142–55, here 150.
40. Mother Teresa, *Essential Writings*, ed. Jean Maalouf, Maryknoll, NY: Orbis Books, 2001, pp. 101–2.

The Ups and Downs, Highs and Lows, and Practicalities of Ecclesiological Analysis with Edward Schillebeeckx

PAUL D. MURRAY

Introduction

This essay seeks to gain some perspective on appropriate ecclesiological method and approach in conversation with Edward Schillebeeckx.[1] It does so, however, not by seeking artificially to isolate one or more explicit ecclesiological methods and associated bodies of extended ecclesiological reflection in his writings and then subjecting them to critique. As other commentators have recognized, such would be a difficult exercise.

John Bowden's short *Portrait of a Theologian*, for example, has no chapter devoted to ecclesiology or Church; neither does Philip Kennedy's work in the *Outstanding Christian Thinkers* series, although here there is a relevant named subsection.[2] Again, whilst the 1989 volume edited by Mary Catherine Hilkert and Robert J. Schreiter, reissued in revised form in 2002 as *The Praxis of the Reign of God*, includes a fine essay by Susan Ross on 'Church and Sacraments', the main twin focus of the essay is on how the sacramentality of the Church and the mission of Church function across Schillebeeckx's theology. Specifically, Ross demonstrates how the focus on sacramentality stretches from an early focus on the Church itself and the Church 's sacramental system as the primary place of tangible encounter with Christ's grace to priority later being given to the Church's call to embody and show forth Christ's witness to and service of the Kingdom of God's justice and mercy in such a fashion as brings the sacramentality of the Church and the mission of the Church into close configuration.[3] As Schillebeeckx himself writes in his Prologue to this volume:

> The trace of God is to be found especially in the face of the rejected and poor person looking at you. I would want to say to all future ministers of God's mysteries – faithful, deacon, priest, bishop, synod, or pope – that the Church is not where you are, but where all the faithful and especially the ministers of the holy mysteries, are, caring and helping, looking into the face of the poor. There is where you see the invisible God 'as passing by'.[4]

The most sustained systematic treatment of Schillebeeckx's ecclesiological work in English is Daniel Speed Thompson's 2003 study, *The Language of Dissent: Edward Schillebeeckx on the Crisis of Authority in the Catholic Church*.[5] Also significant is Pierre Grelot's *Église et Ministères: Pour une dialogue critique avec Edward Schillebeeckx*, as also for the early years of Schillebeeckx's career is Erik Borgman's magisterial study, *Edward Schillebeeckx: A Theologian in His History*.[6]

As regards the place of Church and ecclesiology in Schillebeeckx's own writings: viewed in one way it is omnipresent and recurrent, but one would look in vain for anything approaching a systematic ecclesiological focus and articulation. With the exception of his much discussed and contested works on ministry of the 1980s[7] and his works of the late 1960s on the mission of the Church in Vatican II perspective,[8] there are relatively few explicit, sustained, and methodologically self-reflexive ecclesiological turns in his writings. Whilst the vigilant eye can frequently draw out ecclesiological presuppositions and implications from amidst other concerns, Schillebeeckx's own primary focus generally lies elsewhere. Indeed, whilst the long-awaited and much anticipated third volume to his Christological trilogy had been heralded as intending to deal precisely with matters of Church – as still referenced in its English language title, *Church the Human Story of God* – it proceeds in fact more as a summary of some of the key moves made in the preceding volumes, with the explicitly ecclesiological confined to a chapter advocating a path 'Towards Democratic Rule of the Church as a Community of God'.[9] As he tells us in the Foreword – having first indicated his disappointment with what he experienced as the frustrating of the Vatican II agenda – 'I came to the conclusion that it was better to investigate the heart of the gospel and the Christian religion, its distinctive and unique features, than in a period of Church polarization to be directly concerned with what are really secondary, domestic Church problems. [...]'[10] What he offers instead is 'a bit of *negative ecclesiology*, church theology in a minor key' that seeks to do justice to what he viewed as 'growing throughout the grassroots of the Church as a result of Vatican II'.[11]

In contrast, then, to a more straightforward exposition and analysis of Schillebeeckx's ecclesiological writings, this short preliminary exploration proceeds by identifying a number of sites of continuing tension in contemporary ecclesiology and asking how Schillebeeckx's broader theological options and commitments variously suggest both constructive ways forward in their regard and abiding limitations that need to be transcended. These sites of tension relate to a range of paired differing emphases that can too easily be pressed into stark binary oppositions: between, for example, ecclesiological approaches 'from above' and those 'from below';[12] related to this but not necessarily identical, a contrast between 'high' and 'low' understandings of the Church; in turn, a contrast between more theoretical or doctrinally-driven approaches – focussed on articulating a systematic *understanding* of the Church – and more practical approaches, focussed on furthering the witness and transformative *practice* of the Church;[13] and a contrast between approaches concerned to articulate and promote an ideal of what the Church should be – what Nicholas M. Healy refers to pejoratively as 'blue-print ecclesiologies', which he identifies as having constrained and frustrated too much recent ecclesiological work – and approaches concerned to identify, describe and weigh the lived reality of the concrete Church in all its actual messy particularity.[14]

If for former generations this range of tensions and potential polarities might have been expressed more generally in terms of the relationship between the doctrinal and the historical, for our age it is most likely to be expressed in terms of the relationship between theological accounts of the Church and the varied particularity of lived ecclesial reality as disclosed through empirical social-scientific studies of the Church.[15] This represents the most pressing methodological issue in contemporary ecclesiological work. Seeking to gain some perspective on it constitutes the constructive heart of this essay. In this regard we should once more note that this must be done in a somewhat lateral manner. Whilst in his mature work Schillebeeckx certainly engages critical social theory very closely and gives clear priority to praxis over the abstractly theoretical,[16] it remains that he never really engages with specifically empirical social-scientific studies of the Church. That is, his own primary route into the concrete reality of the Church as means of gaining critical perspective on received doctrinal articulations and interpretations is through historical reconstruction guided by critical social theory rather than the directly empirical and contemporary. To seek progress on this matter through engagement with Schillebeeckx is, then, again to ask what the implications of his broader thought and commitments might be rather than to seek a direct response or fully worked option.

As such, this essay moves through three key phases. First, attention is given to the matter of approaches 'from above' and approaches 'from below' and other attendant issues as they feature in Schillebeeckx's Christological writings. Here it will be seen that far from buying into and reinforcing an unhelpful polarity in this regard, the significant methodological shifts that Schillebeeckx made in the course of his work are best viewed as seeking to hold these perspectives in necessary and appropriate tension. Second, attention turns to how these matters are played out in relation to his specifically ecclesiological writings, particularly so regarding the use he makes of critical social theory as a means of seeking to recover the occluded history of the concrete Church submerged beneath doctrinal narratives shaped by the interests of the holders of ecclesial power and authority. Finally, in a concluding section, assessment is offered as to the relevance of Schillebeeckx's work to our contemporary concern with the appropriate role of empirical social-scientific studies in properly theological analyses of the Church.

I The necessary duality of perspective in Christological reflection

Writing in 1980, after a decade and more when approaches 'from below' in Christological reflection had commonly been given precedence over more traditional approaches 'from above', Nicholas Lash offered a penetrating analysis of some of the confusions variously at work in this regard and of the intrinsic need for an appropriate duality of perspective and method given the character of the central claim at issue in genuinely Christological reflection.[17] As he writes, 'The metaphor [of 'below' and 'above'] is inappropriate inasmuch as systematic reflection, arising out of and not preceding the Christian confession of the humanity and divinity of Christ [. . .] moves between both poles of that confession in the search for understanding' (p. 35).

The point is that if by approaches 'from above' we mean tellings of the story of Jesus from the perspective of God's eternal plan, as in the great creeds and the prologue of the Fourth Gospel, whereas by approaches 'from below' we mean such tellings from the perspective of human experience, memory, and interpretation of the earthly life of Jesus, as, to some degree, in the Gospel of Mark, then in Christian understanding both of these approaches are necessary and, indeed, complementary as their respective presence within the canon of the New Testament itself suggests. In this view, approaches 'from above' can be held to serve the vital function of explicitly drawing out what is implied by the latter and, by so doing, of providing the necessary interpretative preface that authentic engagement with the reality of Jesus came to be seen to require from remarkably early on. As Schillebeeckx writes, 'It is already evident from the New Testament [. . .] that as a man in his full humanity Jesus can only be defined in terms of his unique relationship with God and man'.[18]

In turn, approaches 'from below' can be held to serve the crucial function of constantly returning us to the particularities of the lived, fleshy, genuinely human reality of God's incarnate presence amongst us in the conception, life, death, and resurrection of Jesus of Nazareth. If, as Christian tradition maintains, Jesus really is the embodiment of God's presence amongst us, then the specificities of the life and death of Jesus crucially matter as disclosing to us the actual pattern of God's ways amongst us. Again with Schillebeeckx, 'God can only be defined from and in terms of the human life of Jesus'.[19] Similarly, if Jesus really is the incarnation of God's Word, God's means of self-communication embodied forth in human form, then the particularities of his life are not understood properly until they are understood as 'the transcriptions into the conditions of our existence' of the eternal being in act of God – with profound implications, therefore, for how we are to understand the character of this being in act.[20]

Understood in this way, then, respective perspectives 'from above' and 'from below' on the story of Jesus need not be assumed to equate directly with 'high' and 'low' estimations of the level of dignity to be accorded to Jesus. Whilst approaches 'from above' might be thought naturally to lend themselves to articulating 'high' understandings of Jesus as the unique and unsurpassable presence of God amongst us in fleshly, human form, the Islamic reading of Jesus demonstrates by contrast that it is certainly possible to have an approach 'from above' that adopts a 'low' reading of Jesus as one human being amongst others, albeit an exceptionally gifted human being through whom God communicated. Similarly, as much of the saga around the various quests for the historical Jesus suggests, whilst there might be assumed to be a natural resonance between approaches 'from below' and 'low' understandings of the dignity of Jesus, such is not necessarily the case. From the time of the so-called 'second quest' with Ernst Käsemann onward, much of the most interesting work in Jesus research has been concerned to ask what it was about the human reality of Jesus that led his disciples and the early Christians to make the astonishing claims about him that they did and to trace what links can be seen to exist, if only implicitly, between traditional Christian claims about the significance of Jesus and what actually emerges from an historical reading of the Jesus material.

All of this is helpful in relation to interpreting aright what Schillebeeckx is about in his massive Christological endeavours.

At one level there is a clear contrast between the approach Schillebeeckx assumed in his early work and the one he developed later. His groundbreaking 1959/1963 work *Christ the Sacrament of the Encounter with God* starts out with a fully articulated Trinitarian account of Christ as the second person of the Godhead incarnate: 'The Son of God really did become true man' he tells us.[21] In contrast, the common explicit form of his immense studies in his 1974/1979 work on *Jesus* and his 1977/1980 work on *Christ* is to start out, ostensibly at least, simply with what can be known of Jesus through critical historical reconstruction alone and what this shows about how the early Christian communities variously came to the convictions they did.[22] As we find in the 1978/1980 *Interim Report*: '[W]hat Jesus did so that others began to experience decisive salvation in him, salvation from God, ultimately raises the question: Who is he, that he was able to do such things?'[23]

At another level, however, this formal contrast should not be overplayed. As we shall explore further below, a pervasive commitment in Schillebeeckx's work is to view the dogmatic and the historical as not only compatible but also as necessary correlates. Indeed, Philip Kennedy identifies the 'interplay between universality and particularity' and, in more directly theological terms, the 'mediation of divine transcendence in human, historical immanence' as the abiding concern of Schillebeeckx's work.[24] In the Christological context specifically, the formal statements of traditional doctrine that shape the earlier works can be assumed to be presupposed throughout his later writings even when their avowedly historical form does not make this explicit. That is, as similarly for the vast majority of other Catholic scholars pursuing approaches 'from below', liturgically informed creedal faith and the life of prayer provide the implicit prior frame of understanding, such that historical-critical methods are all along at the service of seeking to understand the character of God's self-revelation in the incarnate Word, Jesus of Nazareth.[25] In his own words, '[I]n all his christological projects a theologian is ultimately a believer, otherwise his project would itself already be meaningless; he is in search of what he can and may in fact believe now, whereas he is a Christian believer thanks to the historical mediation of [. . .] "the great Christian tradition".'[26]

More generally, Schillebeeckx had already fully embraced the recognition in his 1972/1974 work *The Understanding of Faith* that there is no such thing as presuppositionless inquiry; no such thing as hermeneutics that is not in service of, or at least situated within particular interests.[27] As such there is an important sense in which the *Jesus* and *Christ* books, for all their massive concern to attend to and be shaped by the state of scholarly analysis, are rightly to be viewed as both sophisticated works of *a posteriori* apologetics and appropriate attempts to refresh the heart of Christian understanding in the light of what can now be known of the commitments and concerns of Jesus of Nazareth and the earliest Christian experience of him. Viewed in this way, the sustained perspective 'from below' is in service both of showing how Christian communities came to their various perspectives 'from above' and of suggesting how this 'above' (i.e. the embodied and performed divine self-revelation in Jesus of Nazareth) is to be rightly understood and engaged.

Indeed these movements of 'from above to below' and 'from below to above' can already be seen to be conjoined in a fashion in the groundbreaking 1959/1963 work *Christ the Sacrament of the Encounter with God*, where Christ is presented at one and the same time as the supreme revelation of God's offer of love to humanity and 'the supreme realization of the response of human love to this divine offer'; both 'God in a human way, and man in a divine way'.[28] Again, some of the grounds for this non-dualistic approach to Christocentric faith can be seen to have been laid down in the distinctive manner in which Schillebeeckx followed with the mainstream of twentieth-century Catholic theology in overcoming any distorting opposition between the sacred and the profane, grace and nature, by recovering an understanding of creation as brought into being for this purpose; of the world – and human history in a particular way – as the arena of God's grace.

Given the *de facto* prior situatedness of Schillebeeckx's painstaking historically-focussed analyses in the *Jesus* and *Christ* books within the frame of received Christological conviction, and given his understanding of enquiry as always being driven by prior interests, it might strike us – speaking, of course, from our own situation wherein the boundaries between historical exegetical work and theological interpretation are widely and helpfully acknowledged as variously being far more blurred than was assumed to be the case in the 1970s – as having been desirable for Schillebeeckx to have made clearer acknowledgement of this in these works than he actually did. They present as works of ground-up construction wherein their relationship to the substance and articulated forms of received Catholic Christian faith is largely occluded. Whilst this is intended to free the material to speak more directly and cogently to those who come without the presuppositions of Christian faith, the effect, frequently, on the latter is to leave them disorientated and with a sense of having worked very hard to gain fresh perspective on the life, teaching, commitments, and early Christian experience of Jesus without being enabled to appreciate with any ease how this relates to the substance and articulated forms of received Catholic Christian faith. In other words, it could be argued that the assumed perspective 'from above' within which his patient labours 'from below' are situated could well have been both more explicitly articulated from the outset and more clearly integrated in conclusion.

Equally – and somewhat ironically – if one line of criticism of Schillebeeckx's groundbreaking Christological work in his later writings is that he could well have made more explicit and fruitful integrated use of perspectives 'from above', another complementary line of criticism is that he would also have done well to strengthen further his account 'from below' by testing more thoroughly some of the fulcrum positions he adopts. For example, in the context of a basic appreciation for Schillebeeckx's Christological writing, John P. Galvin indicates three areas of possible questioning concerning how felicitous are some of Schillebeeckx's judgements:

Is he correct in his emphasis on the category of the eschatological prophet for understanding the historical Jesus and reconstructing the development of Christology in the early Church? Does his assessment of the crucifixion in primarily negative terms do full justice to the importance of Jesus' death, and to the fact that Jesus' manner of life brought him to this end? Does his treatment of the resurrection as a divine correcting triumph over death's negativity unintentionally devalue the significance of this life?[30]

Viewed in this light, then, Schillebeeckx's Christological work represents a remarkable contribution to the task of developing an approach to Christological reflection and analysis that holds perspectives 'from above' and 'from below' in necessary relation but one that could itself appropriately be stretched and strengthened in each direction.

II As in Christology so in ecclesiology

When we turn from Christology to the subject of the Church in Schillebeeckx's writings, there is again a clear methodological shift of perspective from an unsurprising earlier default toward accounts 'from above' to a later advocacy of the possibility and merits of historically inclined accounts 'from below'. In the 1959/1963 *Christ: The Sacrament of the Encounter with God*, it is 'Christ in his glorified body' who 'is himself the eschatological redemptive community of the Church' as 'both "Head and members."'[31] Again, in the 1965/1972 *Church and World*, 'there is no Church unless in and through Christ.'[32] In contrast, through a series of comparative studies of ministry in different historical contexts and ecclesial periods, the 1980/1981 *Ministry* commits to charting the way in which ecclesial ministry 'developed spontaneously from below [. . .] in accordance with the sociological laws of group formation'.[33] With this, in the 1985 *The Church with a Human Face* he tells us that, as Spirit-indwelt and charism-endowed, there is an important sense in which 'the Church itself is the womb of the ministry'.[34]

As is also the case in the Christological context, however, this shift in perspective represents not a rejection of the force and substance of traditional categories *per se* but a rejection rather of any false 'supernaturalist' accounts that would pose the Church as intrinsically 'alien to the world'.[35] In the 1989/1990 *Church the Human Story of God*, he tells us that '[t]he saving revelation of God, offered to us through and in the Christian experiential tradition of the Church community of faith, is indeed a grace, but a grace mediated through and in the structure of historical experiences'.[36] And again a little further on: 'The Church community as mystery cannot be found behind or above concrete, visible reality. The Church community is to be found *in* this reality which can be demonstrated here and now.'[37] Or as in the 1972/1974 *The Understanding of Faith*: 'The Churches are really the "community of God" and the "temple of the Holy Spirit". [. . .] At the same time, however, the Churches are also historical and contingent.'[38]

As was again similarly the case in the Christological context, in reacting against earlier top-down modes of ecclesiological expression, he again presupposes the continuing force of their basic claim: 'What is described in human experiential terms and sociologically analyzed must ultimately also be expressed in the language of faith. [. . . this] is not in fact a superfluous luxury.'[39] Or as he had put it almost a decade earlier: 'Of course we may not speak about the Church only in descriptive empirical language; we must also speak about the Church in the language of faith, of the Church as the "community of Jesus", as "the body of the Lord", the "temple of the Spirit", and so on.'[40] And in his 1967/1968 *The Eucharist*, it is similarly recognized that the 'sphere of the actively believing, doing and celebrating Church' needs properly to be understood as always already situated within and moved by the prior initiative and gracious presence of the Holy Spirit.[41]

In this manner, Schillebeeckx sets his face both against what he refers to as theological forms of reductionism (which can only understand the Church in terms of its divine foundation and mission, etc.) and against the more familiar historical and sociological forms (that would view the Church purely and simply as a human community).[42] Nor are the experiential, the historical, the sociological, on the one hand, and the theological, on the other, to be viewed as two otherwise utterly distinct languages simply placed uncomfortably alongside each other for purposes of ecclesial and ecclesiological understanding. Rather, they are the appropriate ways respectively of speaking of two dimensions of one and the same reality, which are – in a kind of ecclesial *communicatio idiomatum* – intrinsically oriented to each other, and which, as such, can each be adequately understood only in relation to the other. As he puts it: 'We are always concerned with one and the same reality: the form which has grown up through history and which can be explained sociologically or historically [. . .] is precisely what the believer experiences and expresses in the language of faith as a specific manifestation of grace.'[43] One of his preferred ways of reacting against 'gnostic' and 'dualistic' splitting of 'the mystery of the Church [. . .] into a "heavenly part" [. . .] and an earthly part' is with reference to the statement in *Lumen gentium* §8 that '[t]he earthly Church and the Church endowed with heavenly riches are not to be thought of as two realities'.[44]

As has been alluded to here a couple of times already and as is drawn out explicitly by Mary E. Hines, Schillebeeckx himself is able to overcome any ecclesiological dualism in this manner on account of his 'resolutely sacramental understanding of the Christian community' at the heart of which is his 'profound conviction of the indwelling of the Spirit in the community'. As a consequence, '[h]e is convinced that what comes from below at the same time comes from above. It is precisely through the decisions of the sacramental, human, historical community that God acts in the world'.[45] Or as he puts it himself in *Ministry*: 'The call by the community is the specific ecclesial form of the call by Christ. Ministry from below is ministry from above.'[46] With this and with reference to the liturgical forms that emerged for ordination in the early Church, he describes the 'sense of the community' as meaning 'that what happens in the *ecclesia* is a gift of God's Spirit and not an expression of the autonomy of the Church'.[47]

It should be noted, however, that for all that Schillebeeckx's integrated non-dualistic approach to the life of the Church came to full flower in the period after Vatican II, particularly in his turning to explicitly historical accounts of the Church , this was a move – as again in the case of his Christological work – that was already prefigured in part in his earlier work in a way that would allow for integral and coherent subsequent development. In *Christ the Sacrament*, for example, we find: 'It was the custom in the past to distinguish between the soul of the Church [. . .] and the body of the Church. [. . .] Only too rightly, this view has been abandoned. [. . .] The visible Church itself is the Lord's mystical body.'[48]

Further, the methodological parallels between Schillebeeckx's Christological work and his ecclesiological work extends not just to the balancing throughout of the human and divine dimensions of their respective subjects, of perspectives 'from below' with perspectives 'from above', and to the first members of each of these pairings becoming significantly more pronounced in his mature work. The parallel extends also to the means by which he moves in his developed Christological and ecclesiological writings to give considerably greater attention 'from below' to the human realities respectively of Christ and the Church. In each case the move is made from systematic doctrinally-driven studies to historically-driven reconstructions, both scripturally-rooted and post-scriptural.

That said, he recognizes that the turn from developed, explicit Christian doctrine to scripture is itself no automatic protection from abstraction: 'Even by referring to the proclamation which emerges from the Bible, the Old and New Testaments, we can in fact speak in abstract or speculative terms about the Church.'[49] Again, '[W]e can speak "performatively" about the phenomenon of the "Church"' on the basis of 'a critical analysis of Old and New Testaments and the history of the Church's belief' whilst still by-passing 'the empirical, specific historical manifestations of the Church.'[50]

From the context it is clear that by 'the empirical, specific historical manifestations of the Church' Schillebeeckx is not referring here to understandings of the Church as these might be standardly read-off by the tradition from scripture or church history. He is thinking rather in terms of something that has to be brought into view, retrieved as it were, from behind these standard accounts. When read in the light of the broader movements of his mature thought, it becomes clear that what he has in mind here are the unofficial but real histories of the Church in various contexts and periods which he views as generally becoming submerged and occluded within church history given that it, like history in general, is written from the perspective of those in power and so tends to overlook those who are marginalized from, perhaps even the victims of, the received dominant narratives. For example, in the Introduction to *The Church with a Human Face*, reflecting back on his intentions in *Ministry*, he writes:

> Within the broad tradition of the Church one cannot pass lightly over counter-traditions which are part of the very life of the Church, forgotten truths which are constantly recalled and criticized afresh, and which have a considerable role in theological thematizing. The pastoral intention of *Ministry* was to bring out again the validity of forgotten truths and thus the pauperising of ministry.[51]

In contrast to such ecclesial amnesia Schillebeeckx calls for realism as to all the ways in which, on account of the Church's 'ideological and imperialistic claim to be right', 'alongside all the gifts and favours of a material and spiritual kind which it has brought to many people down the ages [. . .] it has tended to exclude people, cultures, other religions, and [. . .] "alternative Christians", even devastating, destroying and overwhelming them'.[52] In any ecclesiology that seeks to do justice to the lived reality of the Church in history rather than to rest content with theorized, idealized and ideologically shaped abstractions and which seeks to offer transformative repair to these, full account must be taken of these 'often very ambiguous historical mediations'.[53]

Description and understanding alone are not sufficient for this task. Also required is to seek to identify and analyse the various tensions and contradictions that do exist currently and that have existed historically within church practice and with this to seek to identify the various interests that are at stake and to examine the alternative solutions that could be adopted.[54] As he writes: 'In many ecclesiologies, both older and more modern ones, no mention is made of the negative side of the empirical Churches [. . .] or at any rate this side is not made a theme in the theology of the Church. That can no longer happen in our present situation.'[55]

Drawing upon the principles articulated in his methodologically crucial *The Understanding of Faith* of 1972/1974, we might say that in his mature ecclesiological work, Schillebeeckx is more interested in identifying 'what can be and what must be' than in simply describing 'what is'. '[T]he aim of the analysis' he tells us 'is above all an emancipative praxis.'[56] Again, 'In critical theory [. . .] the reconstruction of history is at the service of its interest in a reconstruction of contemporary social relationships and this interest functions precisely as a criticism of those relationships. [. . .] The aim [. . .] is to clear these relationships out of the way.'[57] Correspondingly, a critical theology analyses the models in which 'the contemporary praxis of the Church [. . .] is presented and the attitudes on which it is based' and, 'In correlation with the critical theory of society, it also measures this praxis against its own evangelical claims and thus opens the way for new possibilities.'[58]

The dual poles of accountability and scrutiny in that last point are important. On the one hand, critical social theory and the sociology of knowledge can show '*how* structures of authority come into being in a community and *why* they arise' and how each 'particular culture [. . .] in the long run nevertheless develops towards the specialization and protection [. . .] of its own values and views[. . . .] [I]n this way one can also trace the sociological rules of developments and conflicts between different instances within a cultural community.'[59] On the other hand, however, '[t]he specifically Christian aspect of this criticism of the Church and society comes from a new understanding of Jesus of Nazareth and the kingdom of God'.[60]

Fired then by the tools of Frankfurt critical social theory and a corresponding view of theology 'as the reflective and critical self-consciousness of Christian praxis',[61] Schillebeeckx seeks in his mature ecclesiological writings to recover potentially fruitful but currently submerged and occluded 'specific historical manifestations of the Church ' – relating, for example, to alternative patterns of ministry to those which currently prevail – and so provide potential means of overcoming current problems, such as the now widespread phenomenon of communities being incapable of celebrating the Eucharist due to the lack of an ordained priest. In this regard, at the very start of *The Church with a Human Face* he articulates the concern that drives the entire work: 'The dominant conceptions about the practice and the theology of ministry seem to be robbing the gospel of its force in communities of believers.'[62]

With all of this in view, it should be noted that a possible line of criticism of Schillebeeckx's mature ecclesiological work is that if his central concern is to overcome abstract, overly theorized accounts of the Church by confronting them with the occluded lived reality of the Church at various periods and in various contexts, his manner of proceeding is in its own way still highly theorized. For all his starting out in questions of contemporary concern (for example about tensions and problems in existing patterns, structures, and theologies of ministry) and for all his seeking to analyse and diagnose the back-story to these concerns and to offer constructive redress, he does this through historical reconstructions driven by principles drawn from social-theory rather than, for example, approaches shaped by direct ethnographic observation and analysis of the empirical realities of the contemporary Church which might then be critically contrasted with the theoretical (i.e. doctrinal) self-understanding of the Church in various parts. As he acknowledges in *The Church with a Human Face*, 'Social history presupposes theoretical models in one way or another, implicit or explicit.'[63]

As a consequence, for all his concern to uncover the real particularities of Church history and the critical moves made therein, Schillebeeckx's later ecclesiological work is open to the criticism that it is by no means shorn of its own forms of theoretical abstraction and projection in ways that significantly vitiate the value and accuracy of his analysis at key points. For example, Neil Ormerod points to the way in which Schillebeeckx's analysis of the growing distinction between episcopal and presbyteral ministry in the first two Christian centuries is so shaped by assumptions about the social dynamics of power, patriarchy, and social control and subjection that it cannot find in the emergence of the tradition of mono-episcopate anything other than 'a gradually increasing theological legitimation of relationships of subjection and power which are essentially contrary to the gospel'.[64] As Ormerod comments: 'The theological legitimation of the distinction comes after a process of the centralizing of power, and designates a ranking of that power, which is increasingly focused in the monarchical bishop. For Schillebeeckx, the distinction is little more than an ideological superstructure to support the institutional power relations.'[65]

In the context of reflecting on Schillebeeckx's mature Christological work it was earlier suggested that he could fruitfully have extended his usage both of perspectives 'from above' – in the form of more explicit engagement with the substance of traditional doctrinal understanding of the Jesus of Nazareth – and of perspectives 'from below'; the latter in the form of testing more thoroughly some of the positions he adopts. A similar concern now also pertains in the context of his ecclesiological investigations. On the one hand, for example, as Ormerod highlights, there is need for far greater charitable attention to be paid to the processes of specifically theological discernment that contributed to the emergence of mono-episcopacy in a way that does not simply reduce it in *a priori* fashion to the outworking of social power dynamics without remainder.[66] On the other hand, if Schillebeeckx's concern to overcome theorized doctrinal abstraction and to engage the lived reality of the Church in transformative ways is really to be achieved, then it would be advisable to engage this lived reality not simply through social theoretical analysis and associated heuristic reconstruction of past contexts – all of which surely has a role to play in spite of the criticisms here levelled at the particular ways in which Schillebeeckx goes about this – but also more directly through empirical ethnographic observation and analysis of the contemporary life, structures, processes, and practices of the Church.

In short, for all its many strengths and the significant contributions it has to make to the task of discerning the ecclesiological task, as in Christology so in ecclesiology Schillebeeckx's work needs to be both more theological and more empirical.

III Assessment

Recognizing that we would look in vain for anything approaching an explicit, systematically articulated, and methodologically self-reflexive ecclesiology in Schillebeeckx's work, this essay's probing of the ecclesiological task in conversation with his writings started out by identifying four sites of tension in contemporary ecclesiology: between ecclesiological approaches 'from above' and those 'from below'; between 'high' and 'low' understandings of the Church ; between doctrinally-driven theoretical approaches and more practical approaches; between idealized accounts of what the Church should be and approaches concerned to identify, describe, and weigh the lived reality of the Church as it actually is.

What we have found is that, first, Schillebeeckx makes a major contribution to the holding of perspectives 'from above' and perspectives 'from below' in conjoint conversation, laying down principles that can usefully be adopted in any subsequent work.

Second, we have found that his concern, right in itself, to stand at a critical distance to the received articulations of the tradition and not to allow them to constrain historical enquiry leads him on occasion and against his own stated intentions to tend to give a theologically weaker and more historically and/or sociologically reductionist account of things than is either necessary or fruitful.

Third, we have found that whilst he makes an immense and sophisticated contribution to the task of overcoming forms of theological abstraction by seeking to take the practice of the Church and by articulating an understanding of theology as the critical theory of the Church's emancipatory praxis, he for his own part imposes other frames of social-theoretical interpretation driven by particular interests, which in turn contribute to the above noted tendency at times toward a bottom-up, somewhat reductionist constructivism.

Finally, we have seen that whilst he develops a sophisticated hermeneutic for seeking to engage the submerged and occluded lived reality of the Church in relation to varied historical contexts, the strongly theorized means by which he seeks to do this brings with it its own form of ecclesiological idealism, which again offers an ideal-type solution to the Church's contemporary tensions, albeit one diametrically opposed in some key respects to those offered by robustly doctrinal accounts of the Church. The result is that for all his work being propelled by the need to respond to current ecclesial difficulties, Schillebeeckx ultimately fails to take the complex specificities of our contemporary issues and the full range of constraints as well as possibilities that operate there with sufficient seriousness. As such his reconstruction of lost worlds of alternative possibility – leaving aside earlier noted questions about their accuracy – offers an alternative idealized vision without any convincing pragmatic strategy as to how to travel forward in a way that can genuinely speak to the situations we face and build the necessary consensus around them.

So where does all this leave us in relation to what in the Introduction to this essay we identified as the core contemporary ecclesiological question as to the appropriate relationship between properly theological accounts of the Church and empirical social-scientific studies of the varied particularity of lived ecclesial reality? It is worth reinforcing that the kind of empirical ethnographic studies that are in view here are to be clearly distinguished from the kind of social-theoretical historical reconstructions of the practice of the Church in varied periods and contexts that Schillebeeckx seeks to offer. Whilst, given that it lies outside the specific remit he sets himself, Schillebeeckx can offer us no direct answer to this question, much of what we have found in the course of this analysis of his work is of very definite relevance to the articulation of an adequate answer.

He identifies the need for and shows the possibility of the kind of non-dualistic, mutually enriching relationship between approaches 'from above' and approaches 'from below' that is required if we are to be able to put the findings of empirical social-scientific studies of the Church to genuinely theological use. With this, even if he does not exploit this possibility himself to full or adequate effect, he leaves the door open to situating such empirical studies of lived ecclesial reality within the prior explicit context of a richly and robustly theological understanding of the Church.

Again, the way in which he uses his own proffered social-theoretical historical reconstructions of the Church 's past not simply as alternative descriptions of the Church to be placed alongside received doctrinal understandings but as means of critically scrutinizing the latter – of asking, as he puts it, 'whether the responses given by the Church to God's grace are good or inadequate'[66] – is highly suggestive of the critical role that properly empirical studies of complex ecclesial realities might have to play in testing for the pragmatic coherence pertaining to diverse aspects of received doctrinal understanding of the Church.[67]

In the end, whatever one's assessment of the particular ups and downs and highs and lows of the specific ways in which he went about it himself, the fact that an historically oriented dogmatic theologian of Schillebeeckx's standing could make such a determined effort in relation to the Church to move out of the register of doctrine alone and to seek to engage lived ecclesial reality definitively alters the ecclesiological landscape long-term. We might want to disagree on details; we might even want to disagree on specific aspects of method and appropriate analytical resource, but in the light of Schillebeeckx's controversial ground-breaking labours there can be no credible pursuit of ecclesiological work that rests content with refined doctrinal exposition alone with no reference to the living, breathing, complex and, at times, messy subject that is thereby in view.

Notes

1. In the course of reflecting on this essay, I am grateful for an exchange with Brianne Jacobs, a doctoral student at Fordham University, following the stimulating unpublished paper she offered to the October 2011 meeting of LEST VIII in Leuven, 'From Beginning Above to Starting Below: The Development of Edward Schillebeeckx's Ecclesiology'.

2. John Bowden, *Edward Schillebeeckx: Portrait of a Theologian*, London, SCM Press, 1983; Philip Kennedy, *Schillebeeckx*, London: Geoffrey Chapman, 1993, pp. 69–73 in particular.

3. See Susan A. Ross, 'Church and Sacraments', in Mary Catherine Hilkert and Robert J. Schreiter (eds), *The Praxis of the Reign of God: An Introduction to the Theology of Edward Schillebeeckx*, New York: Fordham University Press, ^{2}2002 (1989), pp. 133–48.

4. Edward Schillebeeckx, 'Prologue: Human God-talk and God's Silence', Robert J. Schreiter (trans.), in Hilkert & Schreiter (eds), *op. cit.*, pp. ix–xviii (xvii–xviii).

5. Daniel Speed Thompson, *The Language of Dissent: Edward Schillebeeckx on the Crisis of Authority in the Catholic Church*, Notre Dame, IN: University of Notre Dame Press, 2003.

6. Pierre Grelot, *Église et Ministères. Pour un dialogue critique avec Edward Schillebeeckx*, Paris: Editions du Cerf, 1983; Erik Borgman, 'Chapter 3. The View of the Church as a Form of the Theology of Culture in the 1950s', in *idem*, *Edward Schillebeeckx: A Theologian in His History*, John Bowden (trans.), London and New York: Continuum, 2003 (1999), pp. 122–90.

7. See Schillebeeckx, *Kerkelijk ambt*, Bloemendaal: Nelissen, 1980, ET *Ministry: A Case for Change*, John Bowden (trans.), London: SCM Press, 1981; *idem*, *Pleidooi voor Mensen in de Kerk. Christelijke Identiteit em Ambten in de Kerk*, Baarn: Nelissen, 1985, ET *The Church with a Human Face: A New and Expanded Theology of Ministry*, John Bowden (trans.), London: SCM Press, 1985. For a constructive alternative proposal to that developed by Schillebeeckx in these writings concerning how best to construe the relationship between lay and ordained, combined with an attempt charitably to understand something of the ecclesial and theological criticism that he provoked in these regards whilst in turn seeking also to maintain his own most significant constructive concerns, see Paul D. Murray, 'The Need for an Integrated Theology of Ministry within Contemporary Catholicism: A Global North Perspective', in Susan Ross, Maria Clara Bingemer, and Paul D. Murray (eds), *Ministries in the Church, Concilium* 2010/1, pp. 43–54.

8. See Schillebeeckx, *Wereld en Kerk*, Bloemendal: Nelissen, 1965, ET *World and Church*, N. D. Smith (trans.), London & New York: Sheed and Ward, 1971; *idem*, *De Zending van de kerk*, Bloemendal: Nelissen, 1968, ET *The Mission of the Church*, N. D. Smith (trans.), London: Sheed and Ward, 1968). In the course of this present essay all quotations from and references to Schillebeeckx's writings are from/to the standard English-language editions.

9. *Idem*, *Mensen als verhaal van God*, Baarn: Uitgeverij H. Nelissen BV, 1989, ET *Church the Human Story of God*, John Bowden (trans.), London: SCM Press, 1990, see in particular pp. 187–228.

10. *Idem*, xiii; also *Idem*, x & p. 209; and *Idem*, *Om het behoud van het evangelie*, Baarn: Nelissen, 1988, *For the Sake of the Gospel*, John Bowden (trans.), London: SCM, 1989, pp. 136–9.
11. Schillebeeckx, *Church the Human Story of God*, xix & xiv; also *idem*, *I Am a Happy Theologian: Conversations with Francesco Strazzari*, John Bowden (trans.), London: SCM Press, 1994, p. 74.
12. The most notable recent example of a major piece of ecclesiological writing premised on a dichotomous understanding of ecclesiological approaches from 'above' and those from 'below' is Roger Haight, S. J., *Christian Community in History Vol I. Historical Ecclesiology*, New York & London: Continuum, 2004, particularly pp. 18–66, a work which, it is interesting to note, is dedicated to Edward Schillebeeckx.
13. 'Christianity is not simply a hermeneutic undertaking, not simply an illumination of existence, but also a renewal of existence, in which "existence" concerns man as an individual person and in his social being.' Schillebeeckx, *Geloofsvertaan: interpretatie en kritiek*, Bloemendaal: Nelissen, 1972, ET *The Understanding of Faith: Interpretation and Criticism*, London: Sheed and Ward, 1974, p. 66; also *Idem*, pp. 132 & 143.
14. 'In general, ecclesiology in our period has become highly systematic and theoretical, focussed more upon discerning the right things to think about the Church rather than orientated to the living, rather messy, confused and confusing body that the Church actually is.' Nicholas M. Healy, *Church, World, and the Christian Life: Practical–Prophetic Ecclesiology*, Cambridge: Cambridge University Press, 2000, p. 3; also pp. 25–51. Healy would entirely endorse Schillebeeckx's comment that ecclesiology 'often proves to be alien to reality': Schillebeeckx, *Church the Human Story of God*, *op. cit.*, p. 210.
15. For a groundbreaking set of UK-based studies in the empirical description and analysis of the actual Church, see Mathew Guest, Karin Tusting, and Linda Woodhead (eds), *Congregational Studies in the UK: Christianity in a Post-Christian Context*, Aldershot: Ashgate, 2004. For an initial essay exploring how such studies might be brought into full theological, ecclesiological discussion and constructive appropriation, see Paul D. Murray and Mathew J. Guest, 'On Discerning the Living Truth of the Church: Theological and Sociological Reflections on *Receptive Ecumenism and the Local Church* – A Regional Comparative Research Project', in Chris Scharen (ed.), *Ecclesiology and Ethnography* Grand Rapids: Eerdmans, 2012 forthcoming; also Paul Murray, 'Serving the Living Truth of the Church : The Task of Ecclesiology in Practice', in Mike Higton and Jim Fodor (eds), *The Routledge Companion to the Practice of Christian Theology*, London & New York: Routledge, 2012 forthcoming.
16. For example in his Prologue to Hilkert & Schreiter (eds) we find, 'Christianity is above all the praxis of the reign of God.', *op. cit.*, xvii.
17. See Nicholas Lash, 'Up and Down in Christology', in Stephen Sykes and Derek Holmes (eds), *New Studies in Theology, 1*, London: Duckworth & Co., 1980, pp. 31–46.
18. Edward Schillebeeckx, *Tussentijds verhaal over twee Jezus boeken*, Bloemendaal: Nelissen, 1978, ET *Interim Report on the Books Jesus and Christ*, John Bowden (trans.), London: SCM Press, 1980, p. 141.
19. *Idem.*
20. Donald M. MacKinnon, 'The Relation of the Doctrines of the Incarnation and the Trinity', in R. W. A. McKinney (ed.), *Creation, Christ and Culture: Studies in Honour of T. F. Torrance*, Edinburgh: T & T Clark, 1976, pp. 92–107 (here 104), cited in Lash, *op. cit.*, p. 39.
21. Edward Schillebeeckx, *Christus sacrament van de Godsontmoeting*, Bilthoven: Nelissen, 1959, ET *Christ the Sacrament with the Encounter with God*, Paul Barrett, O. P.

(trans.) with the assistance of Mark Schoof, O. P. and Laurence Bright, O. P, London: Sheed and Ward, 1963, p. 15; also *Idem*, pp. 56–7, 71–2, 179–81.
22. *Idem*, *Jesus, het verhaal van een levende*, Bloemendaal: Nelissen, 1974, ET *Jesus an Experiment in Christology*, Hubert Hoskins (trans.), London: Collins, 1979; *idem*, *Gerechtigheid en liefde: Genade en bevrijding*, Nelissen, 1977, ET *Christ the Christian Experience in the Modern World*, John Bowden (trans.), London: SCM, Press, 1980.
23. *Idem*, *Interim Report*, *op. cit.*, p. 141.
24. See Kennedy, *op. cit.*, pp. 4, 43 *et passim*
25. I draw here upon what I wrote in Paul Murray, 'Roman Catholic Theology after Vatican II', in David F. Ford with Rachel Muers (ed.), *The Modern Theologians: An Introduction to Christian Theology since 1918*, Oxford: Blackwell, 2005, pp. 265–86 (here 278).
26. Schillebeeckx, *Interim Report*, *op. cit.*, p. 140.
27. See *idem*, *The Understanding of Faith*, *op. cit.*, pp. 57, 63–8, 129–31 *et passim*.
28. See *idem*, *Christ the Sacrament*, *op. cit.*, pp. 14 & 18.
29. John P. Galvin, 'The Story of Jesus as the Story of God', in Hilkert & Schreiter (eds), *op. cit.*, pp. 79–95 (here 93).
30. Schillebeeckx, *Christ the Sacrament*, *op. cit.*, p. 47.
31. *Idem*, *Church and World*, *op. cit.*, p. 145. I am grateful to Brianne Jacobs for drawing my attention to this quotation.
32. *Idem*, *Ministry*, *op. cit.*, p. 5.
33. *Idem*, *The Church with a Human Face*, *op. cit.*, p. 297.
34. *Idem, Church the Human Story of God,* p. xiv.
35. *Idem*, p. 211.
36. *Idem*, p. 213.
37. *Idem*, The Understanding of Faith, *op. cit.*, p. 133.
38. *Idem*, *Church the Human Story of God*, p. 211.
39. *Idem*, *Ministry*, *op. cit.*, p. 84.
40. See *Idem*, *Christus' tegenwoordigheid in de eucharistie*, Bilthoven: Nelissen, 1967, ET *The Eucharist*, N. D. Smith (trans.), London: Sheed and Ward, 1968, p. 151.
41. *Idem*, *The Church with a Human Face*, *op. cit.*, p. 5.
42. *Idem*.
43. See *Idem*, *Church the Human Story of God*, *op. cit.*, p. 211; also *Idem*, *The Understanding of Faith*, *op. cit.*, p. 133; and *idem*, *Ministry*, *op. cit.,* p. 84.
44. Mary E. Hines, 'Ministry: Leadership in the Community of Jesus Christ', in Hilkert & Schreiter (eds), *op. cit.*, pp. 149–66 (here 151).
45. Schillebeeckx, *Ministry*, *op. cit.*, p. 68.
46. *Idem*.
47. *Idem*, *Christ the Sacrament of the Encounter with God*, *op. cit.*, p. 48.
48. *Idem*, *Church the Human Story of God*, *op. cit.*, p. 188.
49. *Idem*.
50. *Idem*, *The Church with a Human Face*, *op. cit.*, p. 6.
51. *Idem*, *Church the Human Story of God*, *op. cit.*, p. 188.
52. *Idem*, xv; also '[W]e cannot live out our own Christian identity here and now except by at the same time explicitly dissociating ourselves from what an ideological kind of Christianity has done to people up to the present time and still continues to do.' *Idem*, p. 189.
53. Compare here Schillebeeckx's description in *The Understanding of Faith* of critical theology's 'point of departure' as being 'the contemporary praxis of the Church ', *op. cit.*, p. 144.
54. *Idem*, *Church the Human Story of God*, *op. cit.*, p. 189.

55. *Idem*, *The Understanding of Faith*, *op. cit.*, p. 114. To clarify, it is not that Schillebeeckx is simply not interested in 'what is' and so just ignores it. Rather his point is that critical theory 'explains its knowledge of what is in the formal sense of what can be and not, for example, in the sense of what must necessarily be or of what ought ethically to be or even of what is eternally valid'.
56. *Idem*.
57. *Idem*, p. 144.
58. *Idem*, *Church the Human Story of God*, *op. cit.*, pp. 210–11, drawing on Peter Berger and Thomas Luckman, *The Social Construction of Reality*, Harmondsworth: Pelican, 1977.
59. *Idem*, 'Critical Theories and Christian Political Commitment', in Alois Müller and Norbert Greinacher (eds), *Political Community and Christian Community*, *Concilium* 84 (1973), pp. 48–61 (here 48).
60. *Idem*, *The Understanding of Faith*, *op. cit.*, xiii; also *Idem*, pp. 143–4 & 154.
61. *Idem*, *The Church with a Human Face*, *op. cit.*, p. 1.
62. *Idem*, p. 41.
63. See Neil Ormerod, 'Ecclesiology and the Social Sciences', in Gerard Mannion and Lewis S. Mudge (eds), *The Routledge Companion to the Christian Church*, New York and London: Routledge, 2008, pp. 639–54 (here 647), citing Schillebeeckx, *The Church with a Human Face*, *op. cit.*, p. 69.
64. Ormerod, *op. cit.*, p. 647.
65. For a significant alternative theo-historical analysis, see Francis A. Sullivan, S. J., *From Apostles to Bishops: The Development of the Episcopacy in the Early Church*, Mahwah, NJ: Paulist Press, 2001.
66. Schillebeeckx, *The Church with a Human Face*, *op. cit.*, p. 5.
67. For further discussion on this, see Murray, 'Discerning the Living Truth of the Church: The Task of Ecclesiology in Practice', *op. cit.*

Incessant Incarnation as the Future of Humanity: The Promise of Schillebeeckx's Sacramental Theology

STEPHAN VAN ERP

Introduction

Edward Schillebeeckx is without a doubt one of the most important figures of the generation of *aggiornamento* theologians who have reflected on theology's new role in Church and Western society in the second half of the twentieth century. With considerable knowledge of the history of theology and the philosophy of his age, he has thoroughly tackled the two main tasks that arose from the new challenges modern theology was facing at the time: *ressourcement* and *renewal*.[1] Schillebeeckx has been involved with most of the work that needed to be done in Catholic theology: debating the various versions of Thomism, understanding the developments of secularization, reflecting on the importance of existential phenomenology for theology, rethinking the Church's place in modern culture, and exploring the historical contexts, worldviews, and experiences that have shaped the Gospels, to name but a few.[2]

Despite the high expectations and promises of this 'new theology' before and after the Second Vatican Council, the re-positioning of theology has been a laborious and polarizing undertaking. Schillebeeckx did not allow himself to be discouraged by this and unremittingly engaged in the renewal of theological content. To him, this was not a correlative strategy of making traditional theology accessible for new generations in new situations. As he saw it, theological renewal was and always will be a necessary response to the ongoing presence of Christ among us, the ever-anew sacramental encounter with God. This means in my view that the *incarnation* should be regarded as the starting point of his theology and its sacramental character as the key motivation of his theological hermeneutics. According to Schillebeeckx, being receptive to the signs of the time primarily meant experiencing God's salvific presence in the world.

In this closing thematic article of this issue of *Concilium*, I should like to explore the future of Edward Schillebeeckx's theology. Since the period in which he developed his theology, theology's tasks seem to have multiplied. Conversations about faith and science, faith and authority, faith and globalization, and intercultural and inter-religious dialogue have intensified. In this diversified landscape of contemporary theology, Schillebeeckx's insights on the incarnation and the sacraments will continue to provide fertile ground for current debates on the God-human relationship in Church and society.[3] Not ethos (Küng), not liberation (Gutiérrez), not the transcendental (Rahner), not glory (von Balthasar), but the *sacramental* will prove to be the key for understanding the relationship between God and people, and the role of the Church in the world as a community that embodies that relationship. In what follows, I shall present a sketch of this theology of the sacramental encounter in the wake of Schillebeeckx's thought. First, I shall describe the sacramental encounter as a foundation of theological hermeneutics. Then, I shall focus on the Christological and ecclesiological implications of the sacramental encounter for our understanding of the human and the secular. Finally, I shall outline the promise of Schillebeeckx's theology.

I History as ongoing revelation: the hermeneutics ofi ncarnation

Although Schillebeeckx's hermeneutics has been influential in Catholic theology up to the present day, it is not the incarnational starting point of his theology that has been taken up by others, nor have its Christological implications. Both Schillebeeckx scholars and critics mention his anthropology and historical criticism, and in particular the contrasting experience of human suffering and the political theology based on it, as the main characteristics of his legacy. But this is, to say the least, a reduction of his thought. Schillebeeckx himself might be partly to blame for this. If we take his contextual (rather than correlational) hermeneutics seriously, we have to recognize that, since the discovery of context and practices of faith as theological sources, theology has constantly needed to reassess its content and stance regarding the time in which it takes place.[4] The expected, but incorrect, conclusion would be that any theology that went before becomes superseded as soon as a new theology is introduced. Is this the tragic consequence of all hermeneutic theology – that theology becomes outdated in accordance with its own principles of perspectivity and contextuality, as soon as the culture that produced it has become a thing of the past? In other words: does the hermeneutics of re-contextualization imply the end of tradition as a productive force?

Schillebeeckx solved this problem by pointing out the double meaning of history, which according to him should result in a double focus for modern theology: On the one hand, modern faith-experiences seem to indicate new theological modes of thought that need articulation and clarification. On the other, a transforming faith forces us to reflect on the renewal that old theological achievements will need to undergo as a result of new influences. This gives modern theology its double focus: both on the past *and* on the future. Schillebeeckx repeatedly emphasized that the truth of past theology will not be lost as a result of the dynamics of a transforming faith, but instead will help to purify and to differentiate, and even, at times, to correct as well. Since the middle of the twentieth century, there has been a growing understanding of the task of systematic theology as explicitly and fundamentally determined by historicity: both in safeguarding old theological truths and in reflecting on the experiences of the historically new as it is immersed in the present and in the future.[5]

What appeared to be a new and promising discovery to Schillebeeckx – allowing the content of theology to be co-determined by contemporary religious experiences and practices – may seem self-evident to the current generation of theologians. Nevertheless, this modern realization maintains its urgency, not only because the diversity of contexts should be taken into account as *loci* where faith comes to the fore, but because there are good theological reasons for taking the present into account as the realm in which the incarnation takes place. However, these current times have become much more difficult to interpret by means of a theological scheme than any before them. Not least, because there seems to be a virtually unbridgeable chasm with the past. This impression of estrangement from theological interpretations in the past may be strengthened by the fact that contemporary theologians feel obliged to bridge that chasm themselves. There is a tendency to consider theology a purely constructive enterprise, instead of believing in the continuity of salvation history, which itself should also be considered as a dynamic that informs and transforms theology. To ignore this might intensify the polarization of contemporary theology in two existing camps that make the same mistake of viewing theology as being purely constructive: a traditionalist one that seeks to safeguard old insights, and a revisionist one that is mainly interested in the content of faith within our modern age.[6]

Schillebeeckx's commitment, from the early stages of his theological development, to considering the interweaving of present and past as the main task of a theological hermeneutics with a view to the future, seems to have become a rare thing in academic theology. In contemporary theology, the hermeneutical problem of the continuity of tradition – i. e. the continuity of revelation – has been dealt with too formally. Contextualization or restoration have become the hermeneutical tools for understanding and confirming our bond with the historical Christ-event, leading to radical particularity on the one hand or new forms of anti-modernism on the other. What is needed, however, is a language for and understanding of that which calls us to contextualize or restore Christian faith. Theological hermeneutics needs to articulate that which commands us to engage with the present as the realm in which God is present with us. To avoid a repetition of previous polarizing theological positions, a reconsideration of the concept of incarnation as the material motivation of theological hermeneutics is called for. What connects the present with the context in which the gospel took shape?[7] How can the promise of God's future be heard in our time? Further study of Schillebeeckx's hermeneutics could articulate this as the ongoing human story of God with his people: God incarnate in our time as the promise and future of humanity.

Some of the next generation of Schillebeeckx scholars are now pointing to the incarnation as a universalizing hermeneutical tool. Robert Schreiter has searched for a new concept of the fullness of faith, embodied in a variety of religious identities.[8] In his radical hermeneutics of tradition, Lieven Boeve has introduced the concept of 'interruption', which, on the one hand, describes God's actions in this world, particularly in a day and age in which the Christian story is no longer taken for granted. On the other hand, this divine interruption of history calls upon people to interrupt the world themselves, which safeguards a full acknowledgment of particular religious, Christian and non-Christian traditions in contemporary society.[9]

Perhaps the best example of the incarnational hermeneutics that could be developed further after Schillebeeckxis the theology of Erik Borgman. In the Editorial to this issue of *Concilium*, he writes that Schillebeeckx 'did not aim at applying or translating the tradition to the present, he wanted to read the present theologically, as a time and a place of God's presence'. Borgman calls his own project a 'theology of culture.' He claims to have derived its statute from Schillebeeckx's early theology, the theology of Marie-Dominique Chenu, and ultimately, that of Thomas Aquinas. What is at stake in this 'theology of culture' is a religious interpretation of contemporary culture, assuming that everything that exists is part of God's creation, and as such, part of the history of salvation. This theology does not regard tradition and the community of the Church as a given that requires interpretation, but as living forms of community that are constantly renewed by God's presence in the world, and as such provide the dynamic, ever-changing subject of theology.[10]

II Christ as sacrament: anthropology is Christology

Does Schillebeeckx's theology suffer from an anthropological reduction? His critics argue that he went too far in founding faith and the tradition of the Church on human experience, and that as a consequence of this, God no longer plays a sovereign role. His emphasis on human experience is indeed the result of a fundamental philosophical consideration argued by modern epistemology and metaphysics and the theological recognition of the social-cultural and historical-political constellation as a main source of reflection. In his earlier works, however, Schillebeeckx always reserves pride of placing for the concept of revelation, and in his later works he increasingly qualifies this term with the concept of salvation. Revelation and salvation, like history, the *humanum* and experience, are central concepts in his theology. The last three have to some extent played a leading role, because – particularly at the Second Vatican council – they were presented to the Church and world of his time as a challenge and as an instruction to modern society. Revelation and experience were not regarded as being hierarchical, as each other's extension, but rather as a symbol of each other, connected and intertwined, but not reducible to each other. The council, and later also Schillebeeckx himself, have without a doubt theologically raised the status of the history of human experience, but always from the perspective of the human as the concrete history of God's salvation – a primarily theological notion, therefore, which Schillebeeckx would go on to provide with a solid but historically dynamic foundation that is inextricably both Christological and anthropological.

Furthermore, one of the most important insights Schillebeeckx obtained from the phenomenology of his time was the anthropocentric notion that human consciousness is a consciousness that has been incarnated in the world and in the body: 'it enters the world by means of the act in which it constitutes itself, in which it presents itself to this part of worldly reality that is our own biological-sensitive physicality'. He used a non-dualistic, constructive concept of the human person's self-realization in the world, outlining the – as he saw them – 'revolutionary' consequences for modern systematic theology, particularly for Christology, for Mariology, for the doctrine of grace, for ecclesiology and for eschatology. He believed that the various and different dogmatic tracts have undergone a radical change as a result of new ideas about the personhood of God and man, the sacramental relationship between them, as well as new ideas about the human experience of the relationship between God and man.

This 'anthropologization' has led to many misunderstandings and debates, as Andrés Torres Queiruga too has discussed in his article in this issue. The main misunderstanding, which has also attached itself to Schillebeeckx's own theology, is that theology now supposedly gains an anthropological foundation and will therefore entirely explain and constitute faith on the basis of human experience, as a consequence of which even theological concepts like revelation and grace are no longer considered the result of divine action, but subjective projections, devoid from any measure of reality. This is an incorrect inference, at least where Schillebeeckx's own theology is involved. According to him, the prime *locus theologicus* is the personal human history of the historical Christ. He believes that the incarnational pivot of the history of salvation must therefore be the precondition of faith and theology.

Experiencing the history of salvation is not just a human project, as it is the result of revelation and grace: God relating to us. This idea of relational salvation involves human persons in such a way that they can freely realize themselves within it. So, even in an anthropologically inspired theology like Schillebeeckx's, the primacy lies with divine revelation in history, even though this is always mediated by human experience. In the 1960s and 1970s, the anthropological focus of modern theology went hand in hand with a growing interest in Christology. Human experience and practices in which the humane comes to the fore were regarded as new events to reconsider the person and work of Jesus Christ. As Johnson Siluvaipillai has stipulated in his article in this issue, the anthropological interest in theology did not therefore result in a moving away from the divinity of Jesus Christ, as far as the theology of Schillebeeckx is concerned. Instead, it pointed to the dynamic and ever-new presence of the history of salvation that has been revealed in the life and work of Jesus the Christ.

According to Schillebeeckx, the first and most fundamental question about human living is that of the mystery of faith, the revelation of the salvific reality of Christ in history, with which we are confronted personally through the light of faith. Through our experiences, we get entrance to that mystery. So the experience of salvation in history tells us the story of Jesus Christ as the Son of God and the Son of man. In short, by drawing the theological connection of human experiences and the history of salvation, Schillebeeckx has not so much articulated that Christology is anthropology – however true that may be – but that the key to true anthropology is Christology.

III The world as sacrament: ecclesiological challenges

Schillebeeckx based the close interconnection between Christology and anthropology on a sacramental view of human history and the present. In the Editorial to this issue, Erik Borgman suggests that Schillebeeckx' theology implied that human history is a sacramental place. The specific sacraments of the Church are sign and instrument of God's presence in the world, and as such, Borgman writes, they make the whole of human history visible as a sacrament of salvation. If it is true, as he suggests, that Schillebeeckx implied that the presence of God's salvation is not limited to the concrete history of Jesus of Nazareth but encompasses the whole of human history up to the present, then further research is needed into ways of viewing the world as a sacramental place. If sacraments are signs and instruments that call for the witnessing and practice of faith, how then do the world and the people that live in it become an instrument of salvation? If the main characteristic of a sacrament is the God-human encounter, how can we discern that encounter in the present? And if such an encounter can be perceived in the here and now, what then is the connection with God's salvific work in Jesus Christ? From a very early stage in his work, Schillebeeckx struggled with these questions.

As early as the 1950s, after his dissertation on the sacramental economy of salvation in the thought of Thomas Aquinas, he further developed his theory of the sacraments in *Christ the Sacrament of the Encounter with God*.[11] In that book's penultimate chapter, on the subject of the Christian life, he tries to connect sacramental and extra-sacramental grace, concluding with a section called 'Everything is grace made visible'. What were his reasons for thinking beyond the sacraments of the Church? Why did he not limit the incarnational presence of God to the historical Christ-event and the mediation of that salvific presence to the visible Church and its sacraments? The answer to that question is partly to warrant the sovereignty of God's Spirit in the world and partly to do justice to present human experiences of the sacramental encounter with God.

Schillebeeckx does not question the significance of Christ as the primordial sacrament, or that of the necessary function of the sacraments of the Church, but he does seek to extend sacrament to the whole of Christian life. In her article, Jennifer Cooper is right to suggest that he identifies a direct connection between Christ and the Eucharist, in as far as Christ himself is given in the Eucharist, instead of it being a gift that refers to him. However, that direct connection does not exclude different forms of mediation. Schillebeeckx writes that although there are only seven sacraments, there are numerous forms of sacramental expression within the life of the Church. It would be wrong to identify the life of the Church with the life that is confined within the bounds of the priesthood and the official sacraments, he argues. It is not exclusively from the sacraments that we derive grace. By this, he did not conclude the opposite, as if the Church and its sacraments were but one, non-necessary form. Merely to concentrate on the invisibility of the Church, rather than also acknowledge that the Church is necessary to make grace visible, would equally be wrong:

> Again and again men have fallen into the heresy of regarding the Church as merely the invisible communion of those who truly live in the union of grace with Christ. They deny the Church its incarnation. They take away not only its weakness and sinfulness but also the visibility of its grace, which means they take away grace itself.[12]

The sacraments however, Schillebeeckx claims, do not primarily proceed from the visible Church alone. They also arise from the 'inward communion of the faithful in grace with Christ our Lord'. In my opinion, Schillebeeckx defies criticism for constructing a social-theoretical ecclesiology, such as Paul Murray's in this issue, precisely because he places grace at the centre of his view of the Church. Moreover, he offers much more than an idealized alternative for the existing Church, as Murray also seems to suggest. Schillebeeckx seeks to balance between an idealized and the existing Church, by calling both the actual sacraments of the visible Church and the sacramental life of the faithful 'ecclesial'. The Church is necessary as the visible reality of faith in everyday life, but as such it represents a holiness that is much wider than the visible Church alone. Murray is right to note that Schillebeeckx does not offer specific strategies for the present challenges of the Church. But he does offer the tools to discern an ecclesial holiness that is also invisibly present in the world, in human weakness and suffering. This invisible presence is a call to the Church to make it visible. For the Church itself, hearing this call results in an openness to ever and anew become Church. This is why Schillebeeckx might have wanted to identify the world as a sacrament: not just because it is the place of deified creaturehood, but because it is also where the ongoing encounter with God takes place in human experiences and human living. Incarnation is not only the event of the gift of God in Christ and the new creation, but also of the incessant giving of God in every individual's life in the here and now.

There is an ambiguity here in Schillebeeckx's theological position on the world being a sacrament and the consequence of the – instrumental – role of the believer. Does that role, as a response to the deification by grace in creation, consist primarily of being sacramentally aware of grace, or of being actively and ethically involved in making visible that the world is given by God's grace? It remains a matter of speculation whether Schillebeeckx, had he further developed his sacramental theology in new directions, would have articulated the role of Christian ethics as a way of understanding sacramental living, as Ben Kautzer has suggested in his article in this issue. In my opinion, Schillebeeckx' sacramental theology need not be pursued in the direction of explicating Christian action. Instead, it needs to focus on the mystical quality of the sacraments by understanding the human *submission* to the world, being the place of God's salvific presence.

To answer the questions that arise from Schillebeeckx's attempts to extend the sacraments to Christian living and the world, one does not need to confirm that submission to Christ could lead to a virtuous engagement with the world. Conversely, one needs to understand how our being in the world is itself a submission to Christ. In the awareness of the world as a sacramental place emerges the encounter with Christ, the primordial sacrament. This encounter with Christ shapes Christian living, which finds its source in our contrasting experiences of human weakness and suffering. Experiencing and contemplating the history of Christ for us is the key for considering the world the place of ongoing creation and incarnation. In that way, it manifests itself as the visible sign and instrument that offers the Church, and the faithful people who shape it, the opportunity to be captured by God's salvific work. Schillebeeckx writes that

> besides these moments which are decisive objectively, in the life of a religious person, there can be others which are of vital importance subjectively. These extra-sacramental bestowals of grace can in fact raise the Christian to greater heights than the grace received in the sacraments themselves. The sacraments are necessary markers, milestones on the way, so that by living the Christian life as a whole we may become more and more one with Christ.[13]

IV Understanding incarnation: theology after Schillebeeckx

The extent of Schillebeeckx's influence on theology is not undisputed. Some regard his thought as a necessary transformation for the twentieth century, which is now not needed any more. They consider him to be an adherent of the liberal theology that is now supposed to have failed: too partial to the historical-critical method and too concerned with the adaptation of Christian faith to the spirit of the times. In contemporary theology, this is the dominant view of Edward Schillebeeckx: a liberal, modern theologian who, open to human experience and cultural context, has adapted theology to the modern age; someone who paid more attention to the history of man than to the eternity of God; a theologian of practice, rather than of theory.

After Schillebeeckx, those polarizing filters based on criteria such as the importance of experience, practice, and history have split theology into different schools and movements. This compartmentalization has also had consequences for the positioning of individual theologians. Schillebeeckx was deemed to belong to the liberal wing, which meant that his work would be received by either a liberal sympathizer or a critical opponent. It meant that, in the era after the criticism of ideology, theology became more and more ideological. Theology after Schillebeeckx became politicized to such an extent that prior to expressing a theological opinion, a fundamental theological self-identification was required. The main question was whether or not one was an orthodox or a liberal, a foundational or a post-foundational, an analytic or a hermeneutic, a historical critic or a diachronic one, a scholarly or an ecclesiastical, a traditional or a modern, etcetera. Such an imposition of one's position leads to an unfortunate reductionism when applied to a theologian such as Schillebeeckx, because such categorizations of his theology do not do justice to his work.

Many theologians are indebted to the historical, anthropological, and critical methods of thinkers like Schillebeeckx, but only few current theologians realize that these methods had a theological, incarnational foundation, as I have shown in this article. The result is a theology after Schillebeeckx that tries to relate to contemporary culture, just as he himself once did. A new generation of theologians tries to find 'the theological' in culture, without actually knowing what to look for and where to look for it. This leads some to conclude that the theological voice is absent in modern culture, and not without reason. Others do see crude analogies of faith in modern cultural expressions and life styles, but they base those analogies on language and on phenomena, instead of on a theological theory of revelation in history, as Schillebeeckx did. When we want to discern the visibility of grace in our present time, we need to look beyond these phenomena and analogies and see the incarnational presence of God in the language and phenomena of today. Schillebeeckx's views of ongoing salvation in history and the world as a sacrament of the encounter with God will prove to be fruitful ideas to pursue if we are to understand this.

How do we continue to build on the work of Schillebeeckx, who focussed his theology on the incarnation and the sacramental encounter with God that people experience in contemporary culture? He has left us a theological heritage that is very rich with materials and reflections, a heritage that urgently requires further investigation. Meanwhile, there have been over 80 doctoral theses on his work, and it seems likely that more are yet to follow. An eleven-volume collection of his works in English will soon be published, and it is likely that this will generate further research as well.[14] That future research partly concerns his own theology: What exactly was his role and importance during and after the Second Vatican Council? In what way did Edward Schillebeeckx's lectures and articles influence the documents of the Council? In what way did his interpretation of those council documents influence his later theological hermeneutics and ecclesiology? What is the importance of his sacramental view of Church and world, and of ministry?

But his work could also play an integral part in future theological research concerning current issues in Church and society: What is the meaning of his theology of the universality of Christ in a religiously pluralistic culture? Has his emphasis on historicity, spirituality, and experiences of suffering changed the study of religion and of faith? How does his form of orthodoxy, orthopraxis, in his words 'the sought-after *humanum*, promised to us in Christ, which has to be performed', relate to the current re-emergence of fundamentalism and neo-orthodoxy in theology and in religion?

Schillebeeckx has allowed his theological agenda to be determined by the present. In keeping with the spirit of the Council, he considered the present to be the time and the place in which God's creation is continued, in which scripture and tradition are continued in new forms and in a new language, and in which the relationship between God and humanity gains a future. According to Schillebeeckx, this present is the key motive of modern theology. In the present, the Word of God can be heard in creation, scripture, and the living language of tradition and faith. Following the directions he has given us, the future of theology should not primarily be concerned with how to reform the Church or the liturgy, or how to live the Christian life. First and foremost, it needs to see and think the visible presence of grace, as it is embodied in the world, and from there necessarily also in the Church and in Christian life. The task of theology is to understand how human life submits to the intimacy of God with us, the incessant incarnation in history. Thus, it will play its own, sacramental part in the history of a positive and creative force that undoubtedly will result in reforms and transformations that are directed toward the future of God.

Notes

1. Cf. Ted Schoof, *Aggiornamento: de doorbraak van een nieuwe katholieke theologie*, Baarn: Het Wereldvenster, 1968, pp. 13–20; ET Mark Schoof (trans.), *Breakthrough: The Beginnings of the New Catholic Theology,* Dublin: Gill and Macmillan, 1970.
2. A collection of his *Concilium* essays can be found in Edward Schillebeeckx, *The Language of Faith: Essays on Jesus, Theology, and the Church*, intro. Robert J. Schreiter, Maryknoll, NY: Orbis Books, 1995.
3. Cf. Lieven Boeve, Frederiek Depoortere, Stephan van Erp (eds), *Edward Schillebeeckx and Contemporary Theology*, New York & London: T&T Clark, 2010.
4. This was the topic of his valedictory lecture: Edward Schillebeeckx, *Theologisch geloofsverstaan anno 1983*, Baarn: Nelissen, 1983.
5. He unfolded his idea of the tasks of systematic theology in an article in the very first issue of his own journal *Tijdschrift voor Theologie*: Edward Schillebeeckx, 'De nieuwe wending in de huidige Dogmatiek', *Tijdschrift voor Theologie* 1 (1961), pp. 17–47.
6. Stephan van Erp, 'Incarnational Theology. Systematic Theology After Schillebeeckx', in Thomas Eggensperger, Ulrich Engel, Angel Mendez-Montoya (eds), *Edward Schillebeeckx. Impulse für Theologien – Impetus Towards Theologies*, Ostfildern: Grünewald Verlag, 2012, pp. 52–65.
7. The 'equals' sign in Schillebeeckx's diagram for the hermeneutics of revelation needs further study. Until now, the proportional relation between gospel and context has become common knowledge in liberal theology, but the continuity between these historical proportionalities has been neglected, not least by Schillebeeckx himself: Edward Schillebeeckx, *Church the Human Story of God*, New York: Crossroad, 1990, pp. 40–5 (diagram on p. 42).
8. Robert Schreiter, *The New Catholicity: Theology between the Global and the Local*, Maryknoll, NY: Orbis Books, 1997, pp. 127–33.
9. Lieven Boeve, *Interrupting Tradition: An Essay on Christian Faith in a Postmodern Context*, Leuven & Dudley, MA: Peeters Press/W. B. Eerdmans, 2003.
10. Erik Borgman, *Edward Schillebeeckx: A Theologian in His History* Part 1: *A Catholic Theology of Culture (1914–1965),* London & New York: Continuum, 2003, pp. 360–81: 'Postscript: Notes on the Theological Yield'; cf. also his '". . . like a sacrament": Towards a Theological View on the Real Existing Church', in Thomas Eggensperger, Ulrich Engel, Angel Mendez-Montoya (eds), *Edward Schillebeeckx: Impulse für Theologien,* pp. 330–51. Borgman presented an outline for his theological program in Dutch: . . . *want de plaats waarop je staat is heilige grond: God als onderzoeksgprogramma,* Amsterdam: Boom, 2008.

11. Edward Schillebeeckx, *Christ the Sacrament of the Encounter with God*, London: Sheed and Ward, 1963.
12. *Idem*, p. 203.
13. *Idem*, p. 200.
14. Edward Schillebeeckx, *Collected Works*, Volumes 1–11, Series Editors: Ted Schoof, Carl Sterkens with Erik Borgman and Robert Schreiter, New York & London: Continuum, 2012.

Part Two: Theological Forum

The Power behind the New English Translation of the Roman Missal

KEVIN T. KELLY

On the Sunday following Mubarak's stepping down as President of Egypt, I made the following point in my homily to the community of Notre Dame Sisters with whom I am privileged to share the Eucharist each day.

> Re-reading the first paragraph of Benedict's 2009 social encyclical, *Caritas in Veritate*, has helped me to see beneath the surface of what has been happening in Tahrir Square. Benedict writes: 'Love is an extraordinary force which leads people to opt for courageous and generous engagement in the field of Justice and Peace.' He goes on to stress that this force 'has its origin in God' and is a 'vocation planted by God in the heart and mind of every human person'. The crowd in Tahrir Square were mainly Muslims but also included many secularists and Coptic Christians. They showed 'courageous and generous engagement in the field of justice and peace' in their peaceful demands for a peaceful, non-violent transition to genuine human freedom and justice. Benedict's amazing words applied to them and made me very conscious that what I was seeing on TV was God's spirit present and active in these people.

However, I also feel that this 'extraordinary force' is manifesting itself as well in the growing unease about the imposition of the new translation of the Roman Missal. A grass-roots resistance seems to be growing among ordinary Catholics who are deeply concerned at the impact this new translation will have on their Sunday Mass. They had no say in what is happening. They feel disempowered. To my mind, their instinct is right. The New Missal imposition is just one instance of the abuse of power in our Church. It is just the tip of the iceberg. I sense a growing discontent among many very committed Catholics who have a deep love for the Church. They feel it is losing touch with the Spirit-inspired vision of Vatican II and its hope for the future. They want to mount a protest against this but there seems no appropriate channel for such protest.

Vatican II placed collegiality at the very heart of church governance. Implied in that teaching is the involvement of all the faithful through collaborative ministry and co-responsibility. The Bishops' Conference of England and Wales made that abundantly clear in 'The Sign we Give', the magnificent 1995 Report from their Working Party on Collaborative Ministry. Sadly, these developments in church governance, so central to the renewal of the Church, have never been properly implemented. That continues to this very day.

I Misuse of power

The flagrant misuse of power involved in the new translation of the Roman Missal is not just about its pastorally disastrous kind of language. It is also about the serious disregard for Vatican II's teaching on collegiality in the process leading up to the New Missal. The original International Commission for English in the Liturgy (ICEL) was set up after the Council and was a fine example of the implementation of collegiality, since it was answerable to the English-speaking bishops' conferences throughout the world. ICEL's only link with the Congregation of Divine Worship (CDW) was the requirement to obtain a '*recognitio*' (a kind of 'rubber stamp'!) for its proposed texts and translations. ICEL was also true to Vatican II's ecumenical spirit since it worked with the liturgical agencies of other Christian Churches to ensure that the common texts and the cycle of biblical readings would be shared in common by the Churches. Moreover, it tried to avoid as far as possible exclusive language which might be offensive to women. These original ICEL texts were carefully vetted and voted upon by all the English-speaking bishops' conferences and are still used today throughout the English-speaking world. However, from the start ICEL had been aware that the need to provide English texts as soon as reasonably possible after the Council inevitably meant that their texts were far from perfect. In fact, Archbishop Denis Hurley, a major figure at Vatican II and first Chair of ICEL, immediately set in motion the work of revising and refining these texts. He gathered together a team of liturgical and literary experts to undertake this task. The guiding principle for their work was based on Vatican II's insistence that the 'full and active participation by all the people is the aim to be considered before all else' (*Sacrosanctum Concilium* 14). Consequently, this team was commissioned to produce texts which, while not being literal word-for-word translations, should be faithful to the meaning of the original, as well as being simple, dignified, and easily understandable. In this they were following the guidance enshrined in the Vatican II-inspired 1969 instruction, 'Comme le prevoît', approved by Paul VI.

By 1998 ICEL's revised version of the Roman Missal was complete and had been examined and approved by all the English-speaking bishops' conferences. It was then sent to the Congregation of Divine Worship (CDW) for its formal '*recognitio*'. This was refused, completely disregarding the key Vatican-II principle of collegiality! Moreover, without any consultation, the CDW brought out an entirely new set of guidelines, *Liturgiam Authenticam*, which insisted on a much more literal fidelity in translating and actually warned against any ecumenical involvement in the process. Moreover, it showed total insensitivity to women by ruling out any use of inclusive language! Archbishop Hurley, by then no longer Chair of ICEL, is reported to have said: 'I find the attitude reflected in the proposed change in translation practice a distressing departure from the spirit of collegiality in favour of authoritative imposition'. He even wrote to a friend: 'At times I find it difficult to understand the attitude of the Roman Curia. It seems to be more concerned with power than with humble service'.[1]

A radically reconstituted ICEL set out to produce a new Roman Missal following the new guide-lines. In due course this was sent out to the English-speaking bishops' conferences. They could have rejected this new Missal but instead chose to approve it. It looks as though they had given up hope of any genuine collegiality. The earlier revision of the Missal that all the bishops' conferences had approved in 1998 was virtually binned, despite being the fruit of years of dedicated expertise and ecumenical cooperation by the commission set up by the original ICEL.[2]

This new Missal has provoked widespread dismay and disquiet, especially among many clergy, fearful of its negative impact on parishioners. For instance, in January of this year the eminent US liturgical scholar, Anthony Ruff OSB, withdrew from a commission given him by the US bishops to help prepare people for the new translation of the Roman Missal in dioceses across the US. In his letter of withdrawal he wrote:

> [. . .] my involvement in that process, as well as my observation of the Holy See's handling of scandal, has gradually opened my eyes to the deep problems in the structures of authority of our church. The forthcoming missal is but a part of a larger pattern of top-down impositions by a central authority that does not consider itself accountable to the larger church. When I think of how secretive the translation process was, how little consultation was done with priests or laity, [. . .] how unsatisfactory the final text is, how this text was imposed on national conferences of bishops in violation of their legitimate episcopal authority [. . .] – and then when I think of Our Lord's teachings on service and love and unity [. . .] I weep.[3]

II What if we wait?

Anthony Ruff is not a lone voice. On 3 February 2011, the Irish Association of Catholic Priests (ACP) issued a press release entitled 'New Translation of the Missal Unacceptable'. They described the texts as 'archaic, elitist and obscure and not in keeping with the natural rhythm, cadence and syntax of the English language' and say: 'from the few available samples of the new texts, it is clear that the style of English used throughout the Mass will be so convoluted that it will be difficult to read the prayers in public'. Moreover, they continue to say that '[i]t is ironic that this Latinised, stilted English is being imposed on Irish people who are so blessed with world-renowned poets, playwrights, and novelists'. They ask the bishops to follow the German bishops who have objected to similar texts being imposed on them and urge them to defer the Missal's introduction for five years to give them time to 'engage with Irish Catholics with a view to developing a new set of texts that will adequately reflect the literary genius and spiritual needs of our Church community in these modern times'.

Two years earlier, an article appeared in *America* (14 December 2009) titled 'What If We Said, "Wait"? The case for a grass-roots review of the new Roman Missal', by Fr Michael G. Ryan. He spoke out of his experience as Pastor of St James Cathedral, Seattle since 1988 and board member of the national Cathedral Ministry Conference. He tells of the reactions of 'disbelief and indignation' of his friends to some of the translations; and of 'audible laughter in the room' at a diocesan seminar for priests and lay-leaders. One reaction will strike chords with many:

> with all that the church has on its plate today—global challenges with regard to justice, peace and the environment; nagging scandals; a severe priest shortage; the growing disenchantment of many women; seriously lagging church attendance—it seems almost ludicrous to push ahead with an agenda that will seem at best trivial and at worst hopelessly out-of-touch.

He also notes that when the new translations were mistakenly introduced ahead of time in South Africa they 'were met almost uniformly with opposition bordering on outrage'. Fr Ryan makes a gentle 'What if?' challenge to his fellow priests:

> What if we, the parish priests of this country who will be charged with the implementation, were to find our voice and tell our bishops that we want to help them avert an almost certain fiasco? What if we told them that we think it unwise to implement these changes until our people have been consulted in an adult manner that truly honors their intelligence and their baptismal birthright? What if we just said, 'Wait, not until our people are ready for the new translations, but until the translations are ready for our people'?

Many Catholics seem to have mixed feelings about the Church at present. At one level they really do love the Church. Yet they also agree with the British theologian Tina Beattie's comment that the problems have not gone away. A lot of these problems are related to the way the authority of God is being used to shore up teaching which, at the very least, is open to debate and, in some instances, rejected as inadequate by many theologians and most people in the Church trying to be faithful to the spirit of Vatican II. I am thinking, for instance, of the rich understanding of human sexuality found in current Catholic and Christian theology, revealing to women and men, gays and lesbians, the depth of their God-given dignity and the ultimate foundation for their sense of self-worth. The same is true of developments in liturgical and Eucharistic theology with its emphasis on full participation, so crucial to the spirit of Vatican II. Using authority to close down these legitimate debates paralyzes pastoral imagination from exploring new ways of coping with such down-to-earth issues as the sacraments to the divorced-remarried, eucharistic hospitality in an ecumenical context, general absolution's highlighting the social dimension of sin, as well as stifling the much-needed debate on contraception, the ordination of women, and the presence of God's love in the faithful love lives of gays and lesbians.

* * *

It seems to be increasingly recognized that abuse of power is also a key factor lying at the heart of the scandal of clerical sex-abuse and episcopal cover-up. The eradication of this horrendous abuse of power seems to lie not just in dealing with the actual perpetrators but also in a radical conversion of the organizational pathology of the Church itself.

Notes

1. Both quotations from Paddy Kearney, *Guardian of the Light: Denis Hurley, Renewing the Church, Opposing Apartheid*, New York & London: T & T Clark, 2009, pp. 292, 295.
2. A full account of this sad and shameful affair can be found in Chapters 4 and 5 of *It's the Eucharist, Thank God*, Decani Books, Brandon, Suffolk, 2009, by Bishop Maurice Taylor who was chair of ICEL during the fateful years of 1997 to 2002).
3. *America* 14 February 2011.

Continuity or Discontinuity: A Methodological Proposal to Study the Theological Contents of the Prayers in the Roman Missal

JOSEPH LIONEL

With the introduction of the English translation of the *editio typica tertia* of the *Missale Romanum* promulgated by Blessed Pope John Paul II in 2002, we are entering into an important phase in the liturgical renewal.[1] It coincides with the approaching fiftieth anniversary of the promulgation of the Constitution *Sacrosanctum Concilium* (4 December 1963).[2] Some of the most dynamic traits of the post-conciliar liturgical reform following the directives of the Council's Constitution on the Sacred Liturgy are observed in the revision of *Ordo Missæ*. Although the *Missale Romanum* promulgated by Pope Paul VI in 1970 and the subsequent typical editions, including the most recent *editio typica tertia* of 2002, radiate the beauty of the Roman liturgy from the treasure house of the prayers, the *Novus Ordo Missæ* has not been free from criticism.

As we stand at this unique moment in the history of the liturgical renewal, we cannot ignore a scholarly approach to answer some of the serious objections raised about the *lex credendi* of the Missal, namely the continuity in the theological content of the prayers. Some of the most drastic criticisms began soon after the implementation of the conciliar directives. For example, in 1969 Cardinal Alfredo Ottaviani, prefect of the Congregation for the Doctrine of Faith, and Cardinal Antonio Bacci, a leading Latin expert who participated in Vatican II, sent official objections to Paul VI accompanied by *Breve esame critico del 'Novus Ordo Missæ'*, a study by a group of Roman theologians.[3]

Ottaviani and Bacci claimed that not just in some details but 'as a whole' the *Novus Ordo* constituted an unprecedented rupture with previous Catholic theology of the Mass. They wrote: '*Novus OrdoMissæ*– considering the new elements [. . .] represents, *both as a whole and in its details, a striking departure from the Catholic theology of the Mass* as formulated at the twenty-second session of the Council of Trent'.[4]

The Council of Trent, in its twenty-second session, taught that the paschal sacrifice on the altar of the cross is 'daily renewed in the Eucharist, in obedience to the command of our Lord'.[5] Ottaviani and Bacci claimed that this reference to the paschal sacrifice of Christ is missing in the new elements of the conciliar Missal.[6]

Similarly, Klaus Gamber claimed that the conciliar liturgical reform had destroyed the Roman Rite.[7] For example, while acclaiming the Roman Canon, the only Eucharistic Prayer in the pre-conciliar Missal, Gamber claims that the introduction of the new Eucharistic Prayers in the conciliar Missal has diminished the importance given to the ancient Eucharistic Prayer. Gamber is certain that 'the new (liberal) theology was a major force behind the liturgical reforms'.[8]

Such criticisms of the *lex credendi* (law of belief) of the post-conciliar Missal are not merely nostalgic: arguments over discontinuity in the Roman Missal continue to this day. For example, Lauren Pristas argues that the post-conciliar liturgical reform has destroyed the beauty of the prayers in the pre-conciliar Missal under the pretext of revision and produced something inferior in quality.[9]

She claims that theological errors crept into the liturgical prayers because of the preoccupation of the reformers with the sensibilities of the modern age rather than the nature of liturgy: 'If the reformers gave priority to the mentality of the age rather than to the justification and sanctification that is accomplished through liturgical incorporation into Christ, [. . .] then we must consider the possibility that theological error lies at the very heart of their work.'[10] She takes the reformers to task for paying too much attention to 'modern anthropology', to the nature of human beings, instead of considering the nature of the Church with liturgy as its self-expression. For example, Pristas criticizes the post-conciliar Missal for de-emphasizing the concept of fasting: 'The word "fast", whether appearing as a noun or a verb (*ieiunium* and *ieiunare*), is found three times in orations of the Paul VI Missal; [. . .] the new Missal uses the word solely in reference to fasting from food. The word 'fast' appears thirty-six times in the orations of the 1962 Missal, where it is used in reference to both fasting from food and fasting from vice.'[11]

Thus most of the critics of the post-conciliar Missal have had both macro and micro problems with the reform. The most important challenge to the *Novus Ordo* by the traditionalists lies in the claim that the *lex credendi* is not expressed in the prayers of the post-conciliar Missal. But, contrary to their claim, Pope Benedict XVI maintains that these two forms (Ordinary and Extraordinary) of the Roman Rite do not deviate from the law of belief: 'These two expressions of the Church's *lex orandi* will in no way lead to a division in the Church's *lex credendi*. They are, in fact two usages of the one Roman rite.'[12] However, it falls to the responsibility of liturgical theologians to study and show how the ordinary form of the Roman Rite does not deviate in its theological content from the previous missal traditions. This study is one small but important step in meeting this responsibility by proposing a methodology to study continuity in the prayers of the Roman Missal tradition.

I What do we mean by continuity?

By continuity we mean the unbroken transmission of the apostolic tradition throughout the Church's history. The subject of continuity arises explicitly only in the debate among scholars in the post-Vatican II context. It attracted renewed attention after the 2005 address by Benedict XVI to the Roman Curia, in which he talked about '*l'ermeneutica della riforma, del rinnovamento nella continuità dell'unico soggetto – Chiesa*' ('the hermeneutics of reform, of renewal in the continuity of the one subject, the Church') [13] and contrasted it with the hermeneutics of discontinuity. Since the term is critical for our study, it is important to have a clear understanding of what we mean by continuity.

Although the documents of Vatican II do not use the term continuity, its sense is implied on several occasions. *Sacrosanctum Concilium* uses the expression *substantiali unitate* (substantial unity) in its norms for liturgical reform as opposed to *rigida munius* (rigid uniformity).[14] That is why the document does not see *legitimis varietatibus* (legitimate variations) as a departure from Tradition.[15] The same document insists that 'sound tradition [*sana traditio*] be retained, and yet the way remains open to legitimate progress [*legitimæ progressioni*]', and 'any new forms adopted should in some way grow organically from forms already existing'.[16] Thus we can conclude that *legitimis varietatibus* is not opposed to the *substantiali unitate* in liturgical reform. Moreover, the Constitution indicates that the substantial unity in the liturgical prayers is directly related to their connection to the Word of God, when it says: '. . . the prayers, collects, and liturgical songs are scriptural in their inspiration and their force, and it is from the scriptures that actions and signs derive their meaning'.[17] This understanding is reiterated in the *Institutio Generalis Missalis Romani* in *Missale Romanum* (IGMR).

The IGMR understands continuity as unity in Tradition: *atque continuam contextamque eius traditionem*, and 'the continual context of the tradition'.[18] The *editio typica tertia* of the *Missale Romanum* is more explicit in its understanding when it articulates continuity as *continua traditione*, 'unbroken tradition'.[19] This articulation by the *editio typica tertia* clearly highlights the thread that links our present prayer to the Christian Tradition.

In the liturgical context, continuity is (1) an expression of the same theological content in the prayer of the Church despite legitimate variations; (2) the intimate connection between scripture and liturgy; and (3) organic development from recent as well as earlier sources such as patristic writings, ancient sacramentaries and missals.

II The three elements of continuity in the Roman Missal

Drawing on insights from the Church's understanding of continuity, this article proposes a three-step methodology to examine continuity between MR 2002 and the Tradition by identifying three elements of continuity in the prayers of the Roman Missal. I choose to call these: substantial, biblical, and traditional continuity.

(1) *Substantial continuity* refers to the unity in the theological content of the prayers from the pre- and post-conciliar missals in spite of some variations. Hence, in order to examine continuity, the researcher will look at the theological content of the prayers from the missal tradition. Although it can be called theological continuity, I prefer the expression 'substantial continuity', because Vatican II itself uses the expression *substantiali unitate*. In this examination I intend to verify whether there

is *fidei immutatæ* 'unchanged faith'.[20] This examination is founded on the thoughts expressed by Paul VI and Benedict XVI. While talking about the post-conciliar Missal of 1970, Paul VI insists on this unity of the Roman Missal tradition in the following words: 'Nothing of the substance of the traditional Mass has been altered.'[21] That is why Benedict XVI can emphasize that the pre-and post-conciliar missals are not two different rites but are two forms (extraordinary and ordinary) of the Roman rite without deviation from the Church's *lex credendi*.[22]

(2) *Biblical continuity* refers to the correspondence between the scripture readings of the day or the season and the words of the prayers with their theological and liturgical significance. Our understanding of biblical continuity is not merely the identification of the same biblical words in MR 1570 and MR 2002 but a study of the meaning of biblical words that are significant in the missal prayers echoing the scripture readings used during different seasons of the year. We should remember two theological principles underlying this proposal to examine biblical continuity: the connection to the history of salvation, and the incarnational usage of biblical concepts in the liturgical prayers. First, biblical words are used in prayers not merely because they are from scripture. They are used in the prayers due to the theological enrichment they bring into the liturgical context.[23] This is shown in the connection between the biblical allusions in the prayers, especially Prefaces and the theme of a liturgical season. That is why identification of the same biblical words in the prefaces of different missals cannot be considered accidental. Such a conservation of the biblical terms in liturgical prayers is a conscious effort by the revisers to show the connection to the history of salvation, which is actualized in a particular moment during the liturgy. Second, our liturgical prayers incarnate the divine word. The fact that the liturgical prayers are shaped by the Word of God, 'grows out of the historical reality of the Word becoming flesh and dwelling among humankind in glory'.[24] That is why mere human words are not capable of giving worthy expressions in the liturgy. Saint Paul wrote: 'for we do not know how to pray as we ought, but that very Spirit intercedes with sighs too deep for words' (Rom. 8.26). Therefore, language inspired by the Word of God is an essential aspect of articulating our prayer. Through this intimate connection between Scripture and liturgy in the composition of liturgical prayers, we

acknowledge the sovereignty of God and the dependency of our human nature.

(3) *Traditional continuity* refers to the connection between the present liturgical texts and the mystagogical writings of the Fathers of the Church and the prayers of ancient sacramentaries. By studying traditional continuity, we can see how our present liturgical prayers are rooted in the prayers of our ancestors in faith. The use of the same source by the two missals supports continuity. In this final step, the researcher will examine whether the prayers of the *Novus Ordo* expand on the orations of the ancient sacramentaries and reflect the mystagogical writings of the Fathers of the Church. If such connection is observed, it will strengthen the argument for continuity and answer the lingering questions about the organic development of the conciliar Missal raised by the critics of the post-conciliar liturgical reform.[25]

These three elements of continuity are to be retained not only in the revision of liturgical texts but also in the translations. For example, while translating into a vernacular the liturgical prayers should preserve the theological content of the original text in Latin as directed by *Liturgiam authenticam*, the fifth instruction regarding vernacular translation.[26]

Conclusion

The continuity that I propose to examine using this three-step methodology is not like making a photocopy of the former text to produce the latter. Rather, the latter text proceeds from the earlier text in an organic development.[27] Just as a runner in a relay race leaves his handprint on the baton that he passes to the next runner, the evidence of organic development and continuity in the texts shows that the liturgical tradition faithfully passes on the apostolic tradition with the mark of every century. Hence, the question of continuity is not merely one pertaining to certain rubrics or a particular word that is missing or preserved, but it is one of fidelity to the faith professed in the Tradition of the Church. Vatican II has taken the Tradition further by enriching the texts based on the ancient euchological sources and opening the Word of God more lavishly to the people. Tradition is at the very heart of the Church, and in each historical context, it tries to vivify and transmit the same. Scholarly studies on continuity, I hope, will assist in the liturgical renewal envisioned by Vatican II and promote unity in the Church, especially in its liturgical celebrations.

Notes

1. Henceforth MR 2002.
2. Henceforth SC.
3. For original see *Breve esame critico del 'Novus Ordo Missæ'*, Rome: Fondazione 'Lumen gentium', 1969), p. 32. See also A. Bugnini, *The Reform of the Liturgy 1948–1975*, trans. M. J. O'Connell, Collegeville, MN: The Liturgical Press, 1983, p. 285.
4. *The Ottaviani Intervention: Short Critical Study of the New Order of Mass by Alfredo Cardinal Ottaviani, Antonio Cardinal Bacci and a Group of Roman Theologians,* trans. A. Cekada, Rockford, IL: Tan Books and Publishers, 1992), p. 27. For original see *Breve esame critico, op. cit.,* p. 32. See also A. Bugnini, *The Reform of the Liturgy, op. cit.*, p. 285. Emphasis added.
5. *The Catechism of the Council of Trent*, trans. J. A. McHugh and C. J. Callan, Rockford, IL: Tan Books and Publishers, 1982), p. 258.
6. 'None of this in the very least implies either the *Real Presence*, or *the reality of the sacrifice*, or the *Sacramental function* of the priest who consecrates, the intrinsic value of the Eucharistic Sacrifice independent of the presence of the assembly. In a word, the Instruction's [IGMR] definition implies *none* of the dogmatic values which are essential to the Mass and which, taken together, provide its true definition.' *The Ottaviani Intervention*, p. 34. See also n. 6.
7. K. Gamber, *The Reform of the Roman Liturgy: Its Problems and Background,* trans. K. D. Grimm, San Juan Capistrano, CA: Una Voce Press, 1993, pp. 24–6.
8. *Ibid.*, p.44.
9. L. Pristas, 'The Pre- and Post-Vatican II Collects of the Dominican Doctors of the Church', *New Blackfriars* 86 (Nov. 2005), p. 609.
10. Pristas, 'Theological Principles That Guided the Redaction of the Roman Missal (1970)', *The Thomist* 67 (Apr. 2003), pp. 185–6.
11. *Ibid.*, pp. 187–8.
12. *Motu Proprio 'SummorumPontificum'*, #1: 'Hæ duæ expressiones "legis orandi" Ecclesiæ, minime vero inducent in divisionem "legis credendi" Ecclesiæ; sunt enim duo usus unici ritus Romani.' Cf. Benedict XVI, Motu proprio *Summorum Pontificum*, 7 July 2007, in AAS 99 (2007), 779.
13. 'Dall'altra parte c'è l'ermeneutica della riforma, del rinnovamento nella continuità dell'unico soggetto-Chiesa, che il Signore ci ha donato; è il soggetto che cresce nel tempo e si sviluppa, rimanendo però sempre lo stesso, unico soggetto del Popolo di Dio in cammino.' Benedict XVI, *Ad Romanam Curiam ob omina natalicia,* AAS 98 (2006), 46 [40–53].
14. SC #37–8 in Tanner, 2:828. For English translation see A. Flannery O. P. (ed.), *Vatican Council II: Constitutions, Decrees, Declarations*, Northport, NY: Costello; Dublin: Dominican Publications, 1995, p. 131.
15. 'Provided that the substantial unity of the Roman Rite is preserved, provision shall be made, when revising the liturgical books, for legitimate variations. . . .' SC #38.
16. SC #23 in Flannery, 127. For Latin text, see Tanner 2, p. 826. See also C. Vagaggini, 'General Norms for the Reform and Fostering of the Liturgy', in A. Bugnini (ed.), *The*

Commentary on the Constitution and on the Instruction on the Sacred Liturgy, New York: Benziger Brothers, 1965, pp. 87, 101.
17. SC #24 in Flannery, *op. cit.*, p. 127.
18. IGMR #1 in MR 1970, p. 19. For English translation see GIRM #1 in LDS II, p. 5.
19. IGMR #397 in MR 2002, p. 60. For English translation see GIRM #397 in LDS II, p. 134. The Instruction *Varietates Legitimæ,* published by the Congregation for Divine Worship and the Discipline of the Sacraments in 1994 mentions *traditioni fidelis* (fidelity to tradition) and *apostolica et continua traditione* (apostolic and continuous tradition). *Varietates Legitimæ* #18, 26 in AAS 87 (1995), pp. 288–314.
20. IGMR #1-4 in MR 1970, pp. 19–26. For English translation see GIRM #1–14 in MR 1970, pp. 17–19.
21. Paul VI, Address to the general audience, on the new Order of Mass about to be introduced, 19 November 1969: AAS 61 (1969), pp. 777–80; Not 5 (1969), pp. 409–12 in DOL, 1759. As we have mentioned earlier, in the Church's understanding, the 'legitimate variations' are not opposed to 'substantial unity'.
22. *Summorum Pontificum*, 7 July 2007, AAS 99 (2007), pp. 779. See note 12.
23. For example, A. Ward and C. Johnson emphasize that the biblical allusions are not entirely repeated in the Prefaces, but the euchological texts 'lightly touch upon it [biblical allusion] in the context of liturgical celebration.' S. Comp., 28. See also C. Barthe, 'The "Mystical" Meaning of the Ceremonies of the Mass: Liturgical Exegesis in the Middle Ages', in U. M. Lang (ed.), *The Genius of the Roman Rite: Historical, Theological, and Pastoral Perspectives on the Catholic Liturgy*, Chicago: Hillenbrand Books, 2010, pp. 180–2.
24. F. Mannion, *Masterworks of God*, Chicago: Hillenbrand Books, 2004, p. 186. See also DV #21, SC # 5–7.
25. For example, Gamber argues against any evidence of organic development in the post-conciliar Missal, because according to him the new Missal changes in essence from MR 1570. That is why this study of continuity in tradition is demanded by the theologians who criticize the *Novus Ordo*, challenging the revisers to show exactly which new text corresponds to which ancient source in order to see evidence of continuity. See K. Gamber, *The Reform of the Roman Liturgy*, pp. 30–4. See also A. Cekada, *The Problems with the Prayers of the Modern Mass*, p. 6.
26. Congregation for Divine Worship and the Discipline of the Sacraments, *Liturgiam authenticam*, the Fifth Instruction Regarding Vernacular Translation, Vatican City, 2001, #20, 22.
27. J. A. Möhler, *Unity in the Church or the Principle of Catholicism*, trans. P. C. Erb, Washington, D.C.: The Catholic University of America Press, 1996, p. 166.

Theological Aspects of the Sexual Abuse Crisis

ERIK BORGMAN

At the end of 2011, a long-awaited report was presented on sexual abuse of minors by representatives of the Roman Catholic Church in the Netherlands.[1] After a long period of relative silence, while sexual abuse in the Church was a topic in a lot of countries around the world, the end of 2009 saw the start of what soon would prove to be a flood of accounts of sexual abuse of minors by representatives of the Roman Catholic Church in the Netherlands, often in the contexts of boarding schools and seminaries. Under the pressure of public opinion, church leaders – the Dutch Bishops Conference and the *Konferentie Nederlandse Religieuzen* (Conference of Dutch Religious) – established an independent committee to investigate what had happened, how it could have happened, how to deal responsibly with what had happened, and what could be done to avoid that it would happen again.

Originally, there was a lot of distrust. The committee, after all, was commissioned by the Church to investigate the Church. Some were calling for a Parliamentary Inquiry. However, the committee chair above all, the ex-politician Wim Deetman, former minister and mayor of The Hague and a Protestant, succeeded in showing convincingly that his committee was independent and in charge of the whole process. It drew up its own plan, was able to do whatever it felt to be necessary, was given all the information it needed, and did not shun drawing conclusions painful to the reputation of the Church. A few days before the report of the Deetman Committee was published, Thomas P. Doyle, a US Dominican specializing in the way the Roman Catholic Church handles charges of sexual abuse and an advocate for its victims, visited the Netherlands. He said in a newspaper interview that he considered it highly unlikely that the report of the Deetman Committee would be objective and without traces of censorship. However, after the press conference at which the results of the investigation were presented and at which he did not conceal that he was impressed by the stories he had heard from victims and by the consequences the abuse had in their lives, Deetman was highly praised by the advocacy groups of victims. They even asked him to lead the process of implementation of the measures proposed by the committee – which Deetman declined.

What has happened in the Netherlands is of course partly due to the specifics in the history of Dutch Catholicism. I will not go into the details. However, quite a few things are typical and related to the self-image of the Roman Catholic Church.

1 Victims and perpetrators

One striking aspect of what in the Netherlands is now called 'the Deetman Report' is that cases of sexual abuse were known by those responsible: bishops and superiors in Institutes for the Religious Life. The issue was even addressed, be it rather primitively and in moralistic terms. However, the emphasis was never on the victims of the abuse, but always on the perpetrators and their moral and spiritual state. This is of course rather serious. Victims were seen by their abusers as nothing but an opportunity to satisfy their lust. And if what had happened to them came to light, they were treated as collateral damage of what was framed as sinful conduct, the instances with which they violated their vow of chastity.

Behind this lies an ultimately flawed theology. Why should it be so difficult for the Church to listen to what seems to be a fairly straightforward statement by Jesus himself?

> An argument arose among Jesus' disciples as to which one of them was the greatest. But Jesus, aware of their inner thoughts, took a little child and put it by his side, and said to them, "Whoever welcomes this child in my name welcomes me, and whoever welcomes me welcomes the one who sent me; for the least among all of you is the greatest" (Luke 9.46–8).

This Gospel passage makes the treatment of children into a central issue for the Church: it is the Church's treatment of Jesus, and through him of God, that is at stake. It is strange, therefore, to consider sexual abuse of minors as simply expressions of individual flaws of Church representatives. What the Church is about becomes visible in the way it treats children. This very insight has always been at the foundation of its special care for orphaned or otherwise threatened or damaged minors.

On top of that, the Roman Catholic Church boasts an awareness of the profound consequences of sexual conduct. The *Catechism of the Catholic Church* states: 'Sexuality affects all aspects of the human person in the unity of his [*sic*] body and soul. It especially concerns affectivity, the capacity to love and to procreate, and in a more general way the aptitude for forming bonds of communion with others.'[2]

That violence in sexual matters can damage human persons in body and soul, as many victims of sexual abuse dramatically show in their life stories, can therefore hardly be a surprise to the Roman Catholic Church. Why, then, did it – and to a large extend: why does it still – not focus on its victims? How is it possible that violating a commandment is seen as more fundamental than violating human persons with whom the Lord of the Church explicitly identifies?

The problem is, I believe, the tendency in Roman Catholic ecclesiology to see the Church as by nature representing divine redemption. In the nineteenth century, the Roman Catholic Church profiled itself as the redemptive force in the midst of a sinful society. In modernity, evil reigned through false claims of freedom and autonomy, the Church claims, but it was the ever-endangered lifeboat riding the waves of turmoil. Although it is not the whole story behind this, the image of Mary's Immaculate Conception is telling in this respect. Mary, who always was the type of the Church in Roman Catholic theology, is presented in the dogma of 1854 as free from original sin. It makes her, and the Church through her, a representative of heaven and of God much more than of the earth and of humanity in their struggle for salvation.

Of course, at the Second Vatican Council the Church officially announced the solidarity of 'the followers of Christ' with the 'joys and hopes, the grief and anguish of the people of our time, especially of those who are poor or afflicted' (*Gaudium et Spes,* 1). However, this did not put an end to the image of the Church as fundamentally *in contrast* to what happened in the world.[3] In this context, it is telling that Pope Benedict XVI wrote in his *Pastoral Letter to the Catholics of Ireland* on the abuse crisis:

> In recent decades [. . .] the Church in your country has had to confront new and serious challenges to the faith arising from the rapid transformation and secularization of Irish society. Fast-paced social change has occurred, often adversely affecting people's traditional adherence to Catholic teaching and values. All too often, the sacramental and devotional practices that sustain faith and enable it to grow, such as frequent confession, daily prayer, and annual retreats, were neglected (no. 4).

The message here is that at the root of the sexual abuse crisis – and at least partially responsible for it – is a turning *away* from traditional Catholicism and its practices, *to* the values of modernity, both in society and in the Church. The evil *comes* from modern society, and the Church is to blame for not being sufficiently watchful in keeping that evil *out of its own ranks*. The question whether for instance the hierarchical structure of the Church itself might be supportive of a tendency to see others of a lower rank as objects to use, instead of as fellow-humans to respect, does not come up and can hardly be asked in this framework.

There is no reason, a separate research survey commissioned by the Deetman Committee confirmed, to think that there is more sexual abuse within the ranks of Dutch Catholic institutions than in others comparable to them. The fact, however, that the Church is *not worse* than other institutions could hardly be an argument to stop investigating why it did not succeed in being *better.* It is the Church's calling, after all, not to be overcome by evil, but 'to overcome evil with good' (Rom. 12.21).

II The Church's self-understanding

The problem that comes with a self-understanding of the Church as being exempted from the works of evil and sin has not diminished in recent years. In the very first year of his pontificate, Pope Benedict XVI stressed that the Church should be understood as 'a subject which increases in time and develops, yet always remaining the same, the one subject of the journeying People of God'.[4] In his view, the Church *has* its true identity and should stick to it, defending it against forces that disturb it from the outside.

This is in significant tension even with what Pope Paul VI wrote in his so-called 'Credo of the People of God', an attempt to summarize the Catholic faith for the period immediately after the Second Vatican Council, dating from 1968. Here the Church is called 'holy, though she has sinners in her bosom, because she herself has no other life but that of grace: it is by living by her life that her members are sanctified; it is by removing themselves from her life that they fall into sins and disorders that prevent the radiation of her sanctity'.[5]

The image here is a Church that *receives* God's grace, which shapes its true identity over and over again, and therefore is able to sanctify its members through the grace given to it. Here the question whether the Church is adequately mindful of the fact that grace has to be *given* to it and whether it has truly been open to the grace, can at least be asked. In Benedict XVI's view the Church has the necessary grace *because* it is the Church, i.e. 'the one subject of the journeying People of God'. Everything coming from the outside appears automatically as a threat to its necessary continuity.

Here, I think, is an issue for more 'progressive' views on the Church as well. In many ecclesiologies written after the Second Vatican Council, the Church is presented as the custodian of the teachings of Jesus. It has to be faithful to that heritage ('more faithful', the message usually is); it has to *return* to that heritage from which it is estranged – the criticism sometimes runs – and then it can actually become the renewing and liberating force in contemporary culture that it claims to be. Although some of the criticism has been highly to the point, and faithfulness to the message of Jesus of course is a major criterion for Church teaching, the pattern in the argument is worryingly close to the one in the ecclesiology of the nineteenth century. The Church is seen as possessing a *depositum* – in the way one has property – and that enables it to be free from the sin and evil with which all other bodies are contaminated. It should try to return to that purity, the argument effectively goes. There has never been such purity, though. Paul already complained that in Corinth 'there is sexual immorality among [Christians], and of a kind that is not found even among pagans' (1 Cor. 5.1). Not even the New Testament is a source only of pure, life-giving water: according to the Christian tradition, the Bible is only the Word of God in an analogous sense. Jesus Christ is the true Word of God, and remains the one who has to renew the Church in the Holy Spirit.

There is no reason to suggest that the freedom of the 1960s made the sexual abuse in the Church increase, as has been suggested. There is, however, also no reason to think that progressive, supposedly less hierarchical-thinking, priests and bishops were less inclined to abusive sexual behaviour. We are truly confronted here with the *mystery* of evil within the very ranks of the Roman Catholic Church. The answer to that cannot just be reform, although a lot has to be reformed, starting with the procedures on how to deal with evil within the ranks of the Church and perpetrated in the name of the Church. The answer has to be, I think, renewal by the only true renewing force the Church can recognize, the living Christ acting in unexpected and unprecedented ways, making 'all things new' (Rev. 21.5). By the way Christ is acting through the complaints, the unsettled and unsettling stories or the resigned silence of the victims of sexual abuse in the Roman Catholic Church, for instance. By the way Christ is acting through new ways of healing that victims' advocates are finding with representatives of perpetrators. By the way Christ is acting through new ways of understanding the Church's redeeming force in a world of sin in which it truly and thoroughly participates.

III A sinful institution

There is no denying that the Church is sinful.[6] In a debate held in Frankfurt in which I participated, on the consequences of this fact for the Church's place in redemption, the suggestion came up that theology should start to take seriously Paul's thesis that 'for our sake [God] made [Christ] to be sin who knew no sin, so that in him we might become the righteousness of God' (2 Cor. 5.21). Obviously this does not suggest moral relativism in any way, as if sin is not evil because Christ became sin. It does suggest, however, God's unconditional solidarity with sinners, because that is the only way to conquer sin truly in order to break away from it.

There is still of lot of thinking to be done here. But representatives of the Church should begin, I feel, with unequivocally identifying themselves as representatives of a sinful institution. Starting from there we could also start thinking of what it means that sexual abuse of minors is so common in a lot of our societies – in the Church and church-related institutions, but also in a lot of other places.[7] According to a survey conducted by the Deetman Committee, approximately one in every ten people in the Netherlands who are now over 45 years of age has experienced some sort of sexual violence from somebody outside of their own families before they reached the age of 18.

Notes

1. W. Deetman *et al.*, *Seksueel misbruik van minderjarigen in de Rooms-Katholieke Kerk: Rapport van de commissie van onderzoek,* Amsterdam: Balans, 2011.
2. *Catechism of the Catholic Church* (1992), no. 2332.
3. K. Rahner, 'Sündige Kirche nach den Dekreten des Zweiten Vatikanische Konzils', in: *idem., Schriften zur Theologie* VI: *Neuere Schriften,* Einsiedeln/Zürich/Köln: Benziger, 1965, pp. 321–47.
4. Benedict XVI, Christmas greetings to the Members of the Roman Curia and Prelature (22 Dec. 2005), at <http://www.vatican.va/holy_father/benedict_xvi/speeches/2005/december/documents/hf_ben_xvi_spe_20051222_roman-curia_en.html>.
5. Paul VI, 'Solemni Hac Liturgia (Credo of the People of God)' (30 June 1968), no 19, at <http://www.vatican.va/holy_father/paul_vi/motu_proprio/documents/hf_p-vi_motu-proprio_19680630_credo_en.html >.
6. K. Rahner, *Schriften zur Theologie.* VI: *Neuere Schriften*, pp. 301–20: 'Kirche der Sünder' (1947). English translation in *A Rahner Reader,* ed. Gerald A. McCool, New York: Crossroad, 1981, pp. 300–5.
7. This essay is a highly abbreviated version of an article published in Dutch as 'Verlossing in nauwe verbondenheid met kwaad: Theologische reflecties over een kerk waarin minderjarigen seksueel worden misbruikt', in *Grensoverschrijdingen geduid: Over seksueel misbruik in katholieke instellingen*, ed. H. Geerts/H. Morssinkhof, Nijmegen: Valkhof Pers, 2011, pp. 13–33.

Contributors

ERIK BORGMAN was born in Amsterdam in 1957 and is professor of systematic theology in the Department of Religious Studies and Theology of Tilburg University in The Netherlands. He is married with two daughters and is a lay Dominican. After studies in philosophy and theology at the University of Nijmegen, he wrote a dissertation on the different forms of liberation theology and their relation to academic Western theology (1990). Between 1998 and 2004, he worked for the Dutch Province of the Order of Preachers to study and keep alive the theology of Edward Schillebeeckx, publishing *Edward Schillebeeckx: A Theologian in his History. Volume I: A Catholic Theology of Culture* (2003). From 2000 to 2007, he worked at the interdisciplinary Heyendaal Institute for theology, sciences, and culture at Radboud University Nijmegen, from 2004 as its academic director. He publishes extensively on the relation between theology, religion, the Christian tradition, and contemporary culture. Dr Borgman is a member of the Board of Directors and Vice-President of *Concilium*.

Address: Department of Religious Studies and Theology, Office D 146,
PO Box 90153, NL – 5000 LE Tilburg
Email: E.P.N.M.Borgman@uvt.nl

JENNIFER COOPER holds degrees in theology from the University of Toronto, the University of Ottawa, and the University of Oxford, where she held the Liddon Research Fellowship at Keble College. She has taught systematic theology since 2004 in the University of Oxford, where she is currently College Lecturer in Theology at St Benet's Hall. Since 2009, she has also taught systematic theology at the College of the Resurrection in Mirfield in conjunction with the University of Sheffield. Her most recent publication is *Humanity in the Mystery of God: The Theological Anthropology of Edward Schillebeeckx* (2009).

Address: St Benet's Hall, 38 St. Giles, Oxford OX1 3LN, UK
Email: jennifer.cooper@stb.ox.ac.uk

BEN KAUTZER is a Ph.D. candidate in theology at Durham University and an administrative assistant at the Centre for Catholic Studies. Previously, he studied philosophical theology at Point Loma Nazarene University and the University of Nottingham. His current doctoral research explores the relationship between ethics, liturgy, and political praxis in contemporary ecclesiology. Focusing on the writings of Louis-Marie Chauvet, his work seeks to develop a liturgical theology of the works of mercy beyond the subjugating cross-pressures of individualistic philanthropy and bureaucratic social welfarism.

Address: Department of Theology and Religion, University of Durham, Abbey House, Palace Green, Durham DH1 3RS, UK.
Email: b.a.kautzer@durham.ac.uk

KEVIN T. KELLY was born in 1933 in Northern Ireland and studied in Lancaster, Fribourg, and Rome. He is a retired Liverpool parish priest and moral theologian, co-founder in 1975 of the Association of Teachers of Moral Theology. In 1980, he made a two-month tour of some third-world countries to experience grassroots liberation theology. 1981–5, Leader of Team Ministry in Skelmersdale New Town; 1985–6, Research Fellow at The Queen's College, Birmingham; 1986–95 combined parish work in inner-city Liverpool with lecturing in moral theology at Heythrop College, London. From 1985 to 2011, he served on the Catholic Agency For Overseas Development (CAFOD) HIV Advisory Committee, visiting AIDS projects in Uganda, Zimbabwe, Zambia, Thailand, and the Philippines. Roman Catholic Parish Priest of shared Roman Catholic/Anglican church in Widnes from 1997 to 2008). Published works include *Life and Love: Towards a Christian Dialogue on Bioethical Questions* (1987); *New Directions in Moral Theology: The Challenge of Being Human* (1992); *Divorce and Second Marriage: Facing the Challenge (New and Expanded Edition)* (1997); *New Directions in Sexual Ethics: Moral Theology and the Challenge of AIDS* (1998); and *From a Parish Base: Essays in moral and pastoral theology* (1999).

Address: 31 Arch View Crescent, Liverpool L1 7BA, UK

JOSEPH LIONEL is a priest of the Catholic Diocese of Thanjavur, Head of the Department of Sacred Liturgy and Catechetics, and Professor of Sacred Liturgy and Social Communication at St Peter's Pontifical Seminary and Institute, Bangalore, India. He holds two master's degrees: one in Journalism from Marquette University, Milwaukee, and another in Library and Information Science from Alagappa University, India, as well as a doctorate in Sacred Theology with specialization in Liturgy from the University of St Mary of the Lake, Mundelein Seminary, Chicago, with a dissertation on continuity in the liturgical renewal through studying the Lenten prefaces from the Roman Missals of 1570 and 2002. He obtained his Ph.D from Thanjavur University, India, with a dissertation on the application of Aristotle's rhetorical principles in the missionary works of Joseph Beschi, a Jesuit missionary to South India. He has written several books on Liturgy in both English and Tamil.

Address: St Peter's Pontifical Seminary / Institute, 61st 8th Main, Malleswaram West P.O., Bangalore, Karnataka 560055, India
Email: jlionel@gmail.com

PAUL D. MURRAY, a married lay Roman Catholic, is Professor of Systematic Theology within the Department of Theology and Religion at Durham University, where he is also Director of the Centre for Catholic Studies. He has previously held posts at St Cuthbert's Seminary, Ushaw College, Durham; Newman College of Higher Education, Birmingham; and within the Department of Pastoral Formation of the Archdiocese of Liverpool. He serves on the British Methodist–Roman Catholic Committee. His first monograph was *Reason, Truth and Theology in Pragmatist Perspective* (2004), and he is editor of *Receptive Ecumenism and the Call to Catholic Learning* (2008). He has also contributed a number of well-received essays to various leading journals and scholarly collections. In June 2006, he was elected to the Editorial Board of *Concilium*. Paul is married to Andrea Murray, the Ecumenical Officer for the Diocese of Hexham and Newcastle. They have two children, Anna (14) and Bede (11).

Address: Department of Theology, University of Durham, Abbey House, Palace Green, Durham DH1 3RS, UK
E-mail: paul.murray@durham.ac.uk

JOHNSON SILUVAIPILLAI holds a licentiate from the Pontifical Urban University, Rome, and a doctoral degree from the Catholic University of Leuven, Belgium. He is currently the Dean of St Paul's Theological Institute, Tiruchirapalli, India, where he teaches courses on Christian sacraments. He is also the editor-in-chief of the Indian theological journal *Vaihara*.

Address: St. Paul's Institute of Theology, P.B: 36, Melapudur, Tiruchirapalli – 620 001, India
Email: john19656@hotmail.com

ANDRÉS TORRES QUEIRUGA was born in 1940, and was till his retirement in 2011 professor of philosophy of religion at the University of Santiago de Compostela. He describes his main concerns as (1) applying the idea of 'the God who creates out of love' to the main theological topics and (2) commitment to an 'evangelically democratic' renewal of church order. His many published works include *Constitución y evolución del dogma* (1977); *Recuperar la salvación* (1977, ^{3}2001); *Creo en Dios Padre* (^{5}1998); *Recuperar la creación* (1997; German trans. 2008); *Fin del cristianismo premoderno* (2000); *Repensar la resurrección* (2003); *Esperanza a pesar del mal* (2005); *Repensar la revelación* (2008; revised ed. of 1977, trans. into Italian, Portuguese and German); *Repensar el mal. De la ponerología a la teodicea* (2011).

Address: Facultade de Filosofía. 15782 Santiago de Compostela. Spain
E-mail: torresqueiruga@gmail.com

STEPHAN VAN ERP was born in Tilburg, the Netherlands, in 1966. He studied theology and philosophy at the Theological Faculty of Tilburg and the Catholic University of Nijmegen. He has taught systematic theology and philosophy of religion at the universities of Oxford, Groningen, and Tilburg. He wrote a dissertation on aesthetics and fundamental theology, *The Art of Theology: Hans Urs von Balthasar's*

Theological Aesthetics and the Foundations of Faith (2004). He publishes in the field of systematic and historical theology, and is a member of the editorial board of *Tijdschrift voor Theologie*. Recently he co-edited *Edward Schillebeeckx and Contemporary Theology* (2010) and *Trouw aan Gods toekomst: De blijvende betekenis van Edward Schillebeeckx* (2010). He is at present lecturer in systematic theology and theory of religion, morals, and culture at the Radboud University in Nijmegen.

Address: Faculty of Theology, Radboud University Nijmegen, P. O. Box 9103, 6500HD Nijmegen, The Netherlands
E-mail: s.vanerp@ftr.ru.nl

CONCILIUM

International Journal of Theology

PUBLISHERS

SCM Press (London, UK)
Matthias-Grünewald Verlag (Ostfildern, Germany)
Editrice Queriniana (Brescia, Italy)
Editorial Verbo Divino (Estella, Spain)
EditoraVozes (Petropolis, Brazil)
Ex Libris and Synopsis (Rijeka, Croatia)

Concilium Secretariat:

Asian Centre for Cross-Cultural Studies,
40/6A, Panayur Kuppam Road, Sholinganallur Post, Panayur, Madras 600119, India.
Phone: +91- 44 24530682 Fax: +91- 44 24530443
E-mail: Concilium.madras@gmail.com
Managing Secretary: Jayashree Narasimhan

Concilium Subscription Information

February	**2012/1:** *Sacramentalizing Human History*
April	**2012/2**: *Theology and Magisterium*
August	**2012/3**: *Vatican II*
October	**2012/4:** *Gender and Theology*
December	**2012/5:** *Water*

New subscribers: to receive *Concilium 2012* (five issues) anywhere in the world, please copy this form, complete it in block capitals and send it with your payment to the dress below.

Please enter my subscription for *Concilium 2012*

Individuals	Institutions
____ £45.00 UK	____ £65.00 UK
____ £85.00 overseas and Eire	____ £105.00 overseas and Eire
____ $135.00 North America/Rest of World	____ $175 North America/Rest of World
____ €110.00 Europe	____ €135.00 Europe

Postage included – airmail for overseas subscribers

Payment Details:

Payment must accompany all orders and can be made by cheque or credit card

I enclose a cheque for £/$/€ _____ Payable to Hymns Ancient and Modern Ltd

Please charge my Visa/MasterCard (Delete as appropriate) for £/$/€ _____

Credit card number ____

Expiry date ____

Signature of cardholder____

Name on card ____

Telephone ____________________E-mail ______________________________

Send your order to *Concilium,* **Hymns Ancient and Modern Ltd**
13a Hellesdon Park Road, Norwich NR6 5DR, UK
E-mail: concilium@hymnsam.co.uk
or order online at www.conciliumjournal.co.uk

Customer service information

All orders must be prepaid. Subscriptions are entered on an annual basis (i.e. January to December). No refunds on subscriptions will be made after the first issue of the Journal has been despatched. If you have any queries or require Information about other payment methods, please contact our Customer Services department.